Master Your Life
101 Transformational
"Quotes"Workbook Series

Lucas J. Robak

www.LucasRobak.com
Lucas@LucasRobak.com
(414) 520-5163

Also available at Amazon.com, LucasRobak.com
Paperback, Kindle, Nook, iBooks, and .pdf

ISBN-13: 978-0-9904403-5-2
ISBN-10: 0-9904403-5-4

TABLE OF CONTENTS

i   Introduction

1   **Chapter One** | Passion

17   **Chapter Two** | Purpose

35   **Chapter Three** | Perception

63   **Chapter Four** | Attitude

91   **Chapter Five** | Fear

111   **Chapter Six** | Failure

127   **Chapter Seven** | Dreams

145   **Chapter Eight** | Goals

161   **Chapter Nine** | Action

221   **Chapter Ten** | Persistence

243   Reference Biographies

263   **About the Author** | Lucas J. Robak

265   Other Books

INTRODUCTION

Master Your Life using Transformational Quotes Workbook Series was written to empower and enrich your life through extra-ordinary words of achievement and success. Use this workbook series as a guide to live your passions, define your optimal outcomes, and take purposeful action while implementing advice from more than 100 exceptional individuals throughout history.

This book is designed to be a tool of transformation. The quotes in this workbook come from some of the world's most enlightened, successful, and inspiring people dating back thousands of years up to the current day. Each quote was selected for its purpose and meaning. Use these quotes to inspire your own thoughts, feelings, and actions.

Master Your Life: 101 Transformational Quotes Workbook is organized into inspirational concepts, one per chapter. You can choose to progress through the book in order, or use the "magic book" technique identified by Richard Bach; hold a problem or concern in your mind and then open up the book at random to be led to the page needed.

Each quote is followed by a suggestion about how to perceive and think about the idea addressed in the quote, with a set of questions. Note: you may have different perceptions and ideas. Feel free to disregard the suggestions offered if they do not feel correct for you. If you find yourself reacting aversely to the suggestion, honor that reaction, notice it, and allow it to lead you to what is right for you. Always do what you think is right.

Take time to contemplate each question before giving a very thorough and specific answer. The questions are designed to lead you to think differently about your life. Give thought to how you might apply the insights you gain. At the end of each chapter are two blank pages for you to take notes and write down other ideas that come to mind.

Take your time! There is no rush to get through this book.

WORKBOOK SUGGESTIONS

Date Each Quote (Day, Month, and Year):
Write the date you start the quote for future reference. This will help you watch your progress through the book.

One Quote Per Day:
Read the quote and the three questions in the morning, then come back to answer them after a full day of thought.

One Quote Per Week:
Every other day, take a different question to think about. Allow for two days, because when you think about the question longer, your subconscious will come up with more concise answers.

Three to Five quotes - Once a Week or Once a Month:
Start a focus group or mastermind group, hire a certified coach, or take the quote to your next class or other gathering to share. Allow for more minds working toward one definite purpose.

One Quote Per Month with Daily Mediation:
Select one quote to focus on daily for an entire month. Give an initial answer to the questions when you first read it. As the days go on, change your answers as you allow the question to resonate within you. It is best if you review the quote and questions every day.

Classroom, Seminar, Workshop, Training, etc.:
Use this book to help inspire your students or clients. When you work in a supportive atmosphere, better ideas will come from these exercises than if you are alone.

Get Creative!:
You may come up with a whole new way that is not mentioned above. Please share your creative genius with Lucas J. Robak on his Facebook or LinkedIn page: @LucasJRobak

BENEFITS OF USING A NOTEBOOK

Some people prefer to use a notebook or post-it notes so they do not write in the workbook. You might want to do this for a number of reasons:

Do It Again:
Repeat the process later without seeing what you wrote before.

Editing:
You can change your answers as you think more about the quote and questions. This helps you until you write out your final draft.

Share or Donate the Book:
Others can experience the inspiration of their own thoughts.

Each chapter contains quotes that pertain to a particular subject. This book is organized in an order which walks you through the process of thinking about your life and what you want it to be. When used mindfully, it continues to build confidence, inspires action, and encourages persistence for when things do not go your way.

Remember: Don't think you need to complete this book in the order that it is organized. Jump around if you would prefer.

At the back of the book is a list of all the people quoted. There you will find a brief biography of each, along with the pages where you can find their quotes. Some individuals prefer quotes from certain people over those from others; there is no judgment for how you want to undertake this process.

Nothing in life is certain except for your thoughts, choices, and actions. Going through this workbook, you will be looking back on your life, at your current situations, and also looking into the future. Your self-talk got you to where you are now and it will take you where you will end up in the future. There are no other factors determining who you will become except for you and the intentions you contemplate.

DAILY LIFE LESSONS

Meditating upon on the quotes in this book will help change your perspective, to enable you to live your life more fully, on a new more conscious path. You will be guided to think about your life in the context of an inspirational quote.

Relationships:
Understand other people and how to effectively communicate with them and yourself.

Health:
Develop the perception necessary to live a healthy lifestyle.

Work:
Promote your thoughts to a new level in order to find your voice and gain influence.

School:
Build success skills which will help you accelerate both in school and, most importantly, beyond school.

Dreams:
Acquire definite precision with your optimal desired outcomes.

As you use this Workbook Series, start noticing what you are saying to yourself throughout the day. Become aware of negative, destructive, diminishing or dissing self-talk. Replace the negative with a more empowering, positive mind-set.

Remember: you are the creator of your own life.

Enjoy this book and all the quotes that come along with it. Share it with your family, friends, classmates, and co-workers to change the world around you!!!

See you at the top!
~ Zig Ziglar ~

This workbook series is dedicated to those who know there is more to life. May these books empower you in your right direction.

CHAPTER ONE
PASSION

Passion: A strong feeling of enthusiasm or excitement for something or about doing something. ~ Merriam-Webster

When you are passionate about your job or whatever it is you enjoy, you are less concerned about your behavior and more concerned about your actions and results. More work is accomplished in less time and with a greater sense of satisfaction.

Thomas Merton said, "Happiness is not a matter of intensity, but of balance, order, rhythm and harmony."

"Keep work work, and life life," said the actor James McAvoy. "It means you've got your life to come back to, somewhere to come home to at night that isn't invaded by your day."

Some people, unsatisfied, carry that unhappiness around with them and create an unsatisfying life at home. Perpetually unhappy, their misery follows them everywhere they go.

Why live life always looking forward to a future moment -- the next vacation, the next weekend, or even to the end of your shift? If you have four weeks of vacation each year, that means you dread 11 months a year and are only happy for one. That is 92% unhappy! We spend way too many waking hours trying to earn a living. It only makes sense to build a life we don't need a vacation from.

Your passion is what you want to do with your life, it is how you will live your purpose. These are your actions which correlate to the bigger picture of your life purpose. Your passion is the vehicle to your own personal destination of success.

By living your passions, you will be more motivated, more satisfied, and healthier than the people who do not like what they do. When you love what you do, it is a passion! Find what you love to do, and do it.

What lies behind us and what lies before us are tiny matters compared to what lies within us.

~ Ralph Waldo Emerson ~

The only things that matter are our thoughts. Nothing else! What you think determines who you are, who you will become, and how you will react. What happened to you is history; you already went through those situations. Your thoughts determine what you learned from those past incidents. What lies within us, our thoughts, determines our future. You can predict the future with your self-talk. You may not know how it will happen; all you need to know is that it will happen. You choose your own destiny. What you think determines your actions. Pay attention to your thinking. Choose your thoughts with care, and you will stand above the rest!

Who is the person I want to become?

_____

_____

_____

_____

_____

When I catch myself thinking about senseless matters,
what would I rather focus on?
(Be specific.)

_____

_____

_____

_____

_____

What future do I want for myself?
What thoughts can I think now which will bring this future to me?

_____

_____

_____

_____

_____

Choose a job you love, and you will never have to work a day in your life.

~ Anonymous ~

When you do what you love, it does not feel like work. Many people believe they have no choice in their work, and that the work is merely a means to an end: to put a roof over their heads, food on the table, and survive. Viewed this way, there is no passion or joy in work when it is only about a paycheck. Other people give up six-figure incomes to make much less because they know there is more to life than money. If you do not love what you are doing, then why do it? Do not sell yourself out for a paycheck. When you do something you love, you will put more passion into it, get more creative, and care about all the aspects of it. When you do what you love, you will never look at it as work.

How do the people in my life who love their jobs make me feel?
How about the ones who hate their jobs?

_____

_____

_____

_____

_____

What are the five things I love doing most?

_____

_____

_____

_____

_____

What career fields can I pursue so I can do what I love every day?

_____

_____

_____

_____

_____

"The more I want to get something done, the less I call it work.

~ Richard Bach ~

Many people have negative perceptions about the idea of work: work is hard, boring, meaningless, dull, a pain, something to endure. Work hurts, tires you out, and drains your energy. Such negative beliefs lead you to hate working. A hateful state of mind is closed. Hate blocks creativity and disables positive passion. Let go of negative associations around work. None of that is true. Work makes the world go round. The truth is, all life is designed to do some kind of work. On the personal human level, work is a virtuous activity which keeps us from making mistakes, provides intrinsic self-worth, and is good for society. Work provides a sense of pride and confidence, helps others, supports families, builds community, reduces stress, helps us sleep better, and enables us to be responsible. Releasing negative ideas opens the door to discovering your passion. You'll know you have found your passion when time flies by. You will want to "work" 80 hours a week just so you don't have to work 40.

The point is, when you love what you're doing, you reap the deep rewards of work. You are always free to choose your thoughts, beliefs, actions. Free to make new choices. Free to live your passion. Many create miserable, hate-filled lives by clinging to limiting beliefs, believing they are prisoners with no choice but to endure pain, boredom, and misery to put food on the table and to buy useless material items which make them only temporarily happy. To get things done and live a life of joy, let go of negative ideas, and choose what you love to do every day.

What do I love doing for hours on end?

_____

_____

_____

_____

_____

How will my community benefit from me pursuing that?

_____

_____

_____

_____

_____

How can I make money doing that?

_____

_____

_____

_____

_____

Do not go where the path may lead, go instead where there is no path and leave a trail.

~ Ralph Waldo Emerson ~

When you take a path which has already been set, it is safe. You will end up where everyone else ends up. You no longer give yourself a choice to develop your own voice and be who you are. A path is there to take you to a predetermined destination which you do not choose; it is where everyone else goes. Yes, making your own path is harder, but you have the power to end up where you want to be. You choose which direction you want to go! Once you create a new path, others will use it too. Be a leader, be your own person, and create as many new paths as you can. Do not accept society saying that this is how you are supposed to do things. You can make decisions on your own and go where you want. Stop letting other people and society control the direction you take in your life. Once you do something different, like living your passion, people will follow in your footsteps.

What results did I produce after creating my own path?

_____

_____

_____

_____

_____

What was my satisfaction level after
doing my own thing and creating my own path?

_____

_____

_____

_____

_____

How can I create my own path in the near future?

_____

_____

_____

_____

_____

Whenever you find yourself on the side of the majority, it is time to pause and reflect.

~ Mark Twain ~

Individuals may be extremely smart. When huge groups of people gather, they move in masses. Masses often end up following individuals who are great at taking initiative. It is natural for people to follow a leader who takes the initiative. However, that leader may be the most incompetent individual to walk this earth. Then the masses are following in the steps of incompetency. Wise people who see the movements of masses question the intelligence of leaders. What groups are you in? Start questioning the leaders in your life; look at their lives and determine if they are worth listening to and following. Never allow the masses to steal your passions!

In what aspects of my life am I following the majority?

_____

_____

_____

_____

_____

What makes me different than everyone else?

_____

_____

_____

_____

_____

What success traits would I like to develop to become who I want to be?

_____

_____

_____

_____

_____

"Two roads diverged in a wood, and I—I took the one less traveled by, and that has made all the difference.

~ Robert Frost ~

As you walk through the woods and see two paths, the one less traveled will have more weeds, bushes, trees, and branches blocking the path. The road less traveled is harder to walk on because there are more obstacles, and it has the potential to be more risky. Each path leads to two different destinations: the path that is clean and unobstructed will lead you to the average person, with average results. The path which is obstructed will lead you to an extra-ordinarily successful life. Stop following the path beaten down by the crowd. Be your own person and follow the road you are most passionate about, the overgrown one with obstacles. Take the road less traveled, take your road!

What happened when I took the road less traveled?

_____

_____

_____

_____

_____

What difference did I make by not following the majority?

_____

_____

_____

_____

_____

What difference can I make in the future by taking the road less traveled?

_____

_____

_____

_____

_____

PASSION NOTES

PASSION NOTES

CHAPTER TWO
PURPOSE

People who have a sense of purpose for their life live longer. Dr. Patrick Hill and Dr. Nicholas Turiano studied six thousand people over fourteen years and published their results in the *Journal of Psychological Science*. The 569 people who passed away during those years reported a lower sense of purpose and less positive relationships than those who lived. No matter what age they were, summarized the *Association for Psychological Science*, people with purpose live longer.

The famous psychologist, Victor Frankl, witnessed the same thing in the Nazi death camps: those who gave up hope and fell into despair, died. Those who created meaning out of their suffering were those who survived.

Purpose comes from our thoughts, actions, and feelings, which determine the meaning and quality of life. It is why we exist, why we get out of bed and skip to our passion.

"A direction for life, and setting overarching goals for what you want to achieve," said Dr. Hill, "can help you actually live longer, regardless of when you find your purpose."

It does not matter who you are or how old you are. If you have a purpose and live it every day, you will have a longer and happier life.

Age is only a state of mind. You have the choice every day to either keep living a purposeful life, or give up and conform. Find your purpose, and deliberately go out and live it every day. The only thing that is stopping you is you.

Do yourself and the world a favor by discovering and fulfilling your life purpose!

The only person you are destined to become is the person you decide to be.

~ *Ralph Waldo Emerson* ~

If you do not believe in destiny, think again. Your destiny is what you choose it to be. The path you are currently on is taking you to the life you are destined to have, but you can change it in an instant. If you look back on your life and the choices you made, you were destined to be right where you are now. If you do not like where you are in life and do not change, you are destined to live your current situation forever. You can choose to be anything you want to be. Every day, you are presented with millions of choices. The decisions you make will create your destiny. Make decisions based on who you want to become, not on who others think you should become!

For what qualities am I destined?

_____

_____

_____

_____

_____

What characteristics do I want to acquire?

_____

_____

_____

_____

_____

What do I want to be known for?

_____

_____

_____

_____

_____

Try not to become a man of success, but rather, try to become a man of value.

~ Albert Einstein ~

Value: Relative worth, usefulness, and/or importance. ~ Merriam-Webster

Your definition of success is unique. Some define success by their bank account. Others define it by their impact on the lives around them. By focusing on becoming a valuable person, by giving and sharing your unique strengths, skills, and gifts, success flows back to you as a byproduct of your own value. Do not always think of how you can benefit from situations; think instead of how you can be of benefit to others. Success comes from helping people, both directly from being appreciated, and indirectly, by putting out into the world what will come back to you. When you are beneficial to others, they will see value in you. Right now, you are important! Prove that to yourself by acting the part. The best way to be successful is to help others become successful. The best way to be a leader is to develop leaders. Stop putting yourself first in all your situations, and be helpful. The value you put out will return to you in abundance.

How do the successful people in my life exhibit value to to others?

_____

_____

_____

_____

_____

How are the people I know invaluable to me?

_____

_____

_____

_____

_____

How can I be more helpful to others?

_____

_____

_____

_____

_____

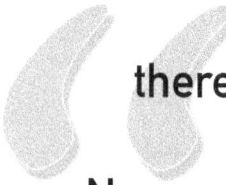

"In my experience, there is only one motivation, and that is desire. No reasons or principle contain it or stand against it.

~ Jane Smiley ~

If you want something badly enough, you will do what you need to do in order for it to happen. Desire causes excuses to disappear. By having a desire for something, nothing will be able to stop you, except yourself. Obstacles become learning experiences, opportunities, and ways to make you grow. Desire will keep motivating you every day. When you fulfill your purpose, the desire to keep moving forward will bring endless energy to complete all the tasks you need to do. You will be doing things you have never imagined before; your desire will be that strong!

What am I currently motivated to do?

_____

_____

_____

_____

_____

What do I desire to achieve?

_____

_____

_____

_____

_____

What stopped me in the past which I will not allow to stop me again?
How will I successfully move past it?

_____

_____

_____

_____

_____

The whole secret of a successful life is to find out what is one's destiny to do, and then do it.

~ Henry Ford ~

We are all destined to do something. If we all followed our destiny, this would be a perfect world. As babies, we know what we want, and will do anything to get it. It is our parents, teachers, friends, and neighbors that break us down and make us conform to society. We all once had innocent minds with dreams of possibility. As we grow up, we are told, "You cannot do this", "that is impossible," "you are not qualified," "you are too stupid," "why would you waste your time with that?","it will be very hard to do,", etc. After years of dream-stealing negativity, we become like everyone else, doing what we are told and what is expected of us.

We are all better than that! Find your passion, find your purpose, seek out mentors, and invest in your personal development with books, courses, seminars, and classes. To live your destiny, follow your gut instincts, and do what you know is right every step of the way!

What was I born to do?

_____

_____

_____

_____

How will I benefit from my results after becoming successful?

_____

_____

_____

_____

How will others benefit after I become successful?

_____

_____

_____

_____

The only thing worse than being blind is having sight but no vision.

~ Helen Keller ~

Vision: Something that you imagine…a picture that you see in your mind…a thought, concept, or object formed by the imagination…the act or power of imagination. ~ Merriam-Webster

Imagine being deaf and blind; that was Helen Keller's life. Blindness and deafness can stop people from living their dreams. But Keller showed the world another way. She chose not to accept these as limiting factors; she saw them as assets. Those who see challenges as assets have vision. When you do not have a voice, you allow life to push you around because you have no ambition to pursue the dreams which you do not have. The greatest people in the world have purpose and vision; they are able to imagine and see the end result as successful. By keeping the successful end in sight, you keep motivated, and that will help you unfold the next step in the process of making your dream reality. Believe your dream is possible, and do not let anyone take that away from you!

What limiting factors of mine can be viewed as assets?

_____

_____

_____

_____

_____

What is one vision of mine I want to see as a reality?
Why?

_____

_____

_____

_____

_____

What does my end result look, feel, and sound like?

_____

_____

_____

_____

_____

> First, have a definite, clear
> practical ideal; a goal, an objective.
> Second, have the necessary means
> to achieve your ends; wisdom,
> money, materials, and methods.
> Third, adjust all your means to that end.

~ Aristotle ~

Start with the end in mind. Figure out what it is you want to become in life. Set goals and have objectives to reach them. Once you know where you want to go, determine what knowledge you should acquire, how much money you will need, the materials you will use, and the different methods you can implement. Once you have all this information, make adjustments in your life to acquire all the means it will take to accomplish your objective. If you do not have the knowledge, start reading, go to trainings, seminars, workshops, and ask experts. If you do not have the money, borrow it, get loans, or use crowdfunding sites like kickstarter.com or gofundme.com. Where there is a will, there is always a way. Figure out the way, and stop at nothing to obtain your desires.

What is my one, clear, practical objective?

_____

_____

_____

_____

_____

What knowledge do I still need to acquire?
Where will I find it?

_____

_____

_____

_____

_____

What options do I have for the different methods I can implement?

_____

_____

_____

_____

_____

"Definiteness of purpose is the starting point of all achievement.

~ W. Clement Stone ~

When you travel, you need to know where you are starting and where you are going in order to know when you get there. Knowing your definite purpose in life will help you decide what goals to set and how to react to situations that arise along the way. Your personal purpose statement is a guide for all the decisions you will face along the way. Your purpose is vital to your success in every area of life. Those who are successful have a definite purpose, whether they consciously know it or not. By knowing why you exist, your decisions, goals, and where to begin will become easy! By discovering your life purpose, you will know what you need to do each day to fulfill it. Knowing why you exist, you will know what to do and how to do it. This is your guide for all your decisions.

What do I believe I was put on this earth to do?

_____

_____

_____

_____

_____

How will discovering my life purpose benefit the world around me?

_____

_____

_____

_____

_____

What is my life purpose?
(HINT: Sum up all previous answers in 35 words or less)

_____

_____

_____

_____

_____

PURPOSE NOTES

PURPOSE NOTES

CHAPTER THREE
PERCEPTION

Perception: The way you think about or understand someone or something; the ability to understand or notice something easily; the way that you notice or understand something using one of your senses. - Merriam-Webster

Naturally, everyone in the world has a different perception of the same things. That is the reason police officers get ten different stories of an incident from ten different witnesses. We all have filters which make sense of reality for us, and these create our perceptions. Know this—your perception of reality is not reality; it is false 100 percent of the time.

Every second of every day, our five senses are overwhelmed with two million bits of information per second which we need to understand. We all take that information and delete, distort, and generalize it down to 126 bits per second. This process of filtering creates our own, false reality of what actually happened.

There is so much information coming in that we need to delete some of it. It is as simple as not recognizing it was ever there. When we distort information, we are seeing, hearing, smelling, and feeling things that do not exist in that reality. This causes us to be the only ones who actually experience that particular sensation. Through generalization, our past experiences are applied to what is happening at any given moment.

We see what we want and/or expect to see.

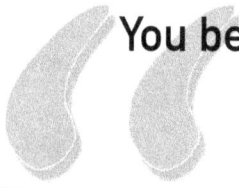

You become what you believe.

~ Oprah Winfrey ~

"Your personal perception of reality is determined by the beliefs you hold," said psychiatrist and personal change expert, Abigail Brenner, M.D., referencing many confirming published studies. Further, you become what you believe. Beliefs are set in us during early childhood by parents, teachers, peers, and neighbors. People can go their entire lives believing or not believing in themselves because of what they learned before the age of 17. If you are a parent, teacher, or any adult figure in a child's life, leave other people's dreams alone. If you are an adult who had a negative self-belief instilled by adults in your life growing up, remember: you have a choice in what you agree with. Just because they believe you are not capable of greatness does not mean you need to believe that as well. Everyone can change, but first, one needs to believe in change. Believe in yourself. You have the power to change your life into whatever it is you want to create. Believe you can, and you will! There is no one stopping you but yourself. If someone tells you that your beliefs and ideas are stupid or impossible, there is no need to ever listen to them again because they are small thinkers. Be a big thinker!

What do I want to believe I can do?

_____

_____

_____

_____

What is the perception I want for myself?

_____

_____

_____

_____

How can I practice believing in myself?

_____

_____

_____

_____

Whether you think you can or think you can't, you're right.

~ Henry Ford ~

When you think something is impossible, you immediately start coming up with all the reasons why it is impossible. When you think you can accomplish an impossible task, you will come up with a lot of reasons why and how you can make it possible. Start building your critical thinking skills. Stop asking "why?" and start asking "why not?" Or better yet, ask "how?" No matter what you think about a certain situation, you are right. If you think you cannot do it, you will never do it, because chances are you will not even try. If you believe you can, you will persist until you accomplish what it is you set out to do. There are no guarantees in life, except for the belief in yourself. Throughout life, negative people will swarm around you and your dreams, telling you all the reasons why you should take the easy way out and do what society says. If you are crazy enough to believe you can change the world, you will change the world! If you believe you will create a tele-porter, you will create a tele-porter.

What do I believe I will never achieve?
Why?

_____

_____

_____

_____

_____

From what I wrote above, give five or more reasons why it is possible!

_____

_____

_____

_____

_____

If I had unlimited resources, what would be my first three steps?

_____

_____

_____

_____

I am not a product of my circumstances. I am a product of my decisions.

~ Stephen R. Covey ~

There will always be circumstances and events in your life you cannot control. You cannot control the weather, natural disasters, media, politics, or people. You can, however, control the thoughts you have and the decisions you make after a circumstance is presented in your life. All the decisions you make create the "product" that is you today. The thoughts you have in your mind determine the decisions you will make when you are faced with any life event. Do not let the events of your life control you. The only things you should be concerned with are your thoughts and actions. This is what makes you who you are! Start making better decisions every moment of every day. Forget the external events in your life, and start living the life of your decisions, because you already are.

What is the "product" I want to become?

_____

_____

_____

_____

_____

What decisions will I be faced with?
(List all I can think of)

_____

_____

_____

_____

_____

What are the thoughts and actions of my ideal "product"?

_____

_____

_____

_____

_____

Remember that not getting what you want is sometimes a wonderful stroke of luck.

~ Dalai Lama ~

You've probably experienced this more times than you would have liked, you cannot always get what you want. True! When you do not get what you want, when you hit a brick wall (an obstacle), it has the potential to make you stronger, and put you in another direction which will benefit you more. You may feel like you hit rock bottom when you do not get what you want; feel lucky, because in the end, it can be perceived as a positive. Believe that only good will come from any situation, and good comes— from even the worst situations. Do not live a greedy, envious life, because you will never be satisfied. People who feel entitled to other people's hard work will never be satisfied, because they will always want more of what they do not deserve. As long as you remember you cannot get everything you want, you will be happier. You can try to get everything you want, but when it does not happen, do not give up. You will be pointed in a different direction, with new and better opportunities than what you originally wanted.

What great thing happened afterI did not get what I originally wanted?

_____

_____

_____

_____

_____

How did I make that a positive?

_____

_____

_____

_____

_____

How can I turn an old stroke of bad luck into a positive?

_____

_____

_____

_____

_____

I attribute my success to this: I never gave or took any excuse.

~ Florence Nightingale ~

Excuses are what our society enables. Give excuses, blame someone else, and complain about the results. Excuses come from the tongues of losers. Start taking responsibility for your actions and your life as a whole. Rationalizing why you did not do something or filing a lawsuit is a lot easier than taking responsibility and blaming yourself. When you own up to your actions, and do not justify your actions, people will notice and look up to you. Most importantly, when you take responsibility for your actions, your subconscious mind will notice. This is very important! When you place blame on others, subconsciously you are giving them control of your life, and you allow life to happen to you. Having bad things happen to you your whole life can force you to see yourself as the victim. A victim is simply a state of mind which you choose. Stop doing that to yourself and take responsibility for your life. No one cares if you are the victim, they are too worried about becoming one themselves. Stop making excuses, and take control of your life. Create your life by taking responsibility!

What do I think when people give me excuse after excuse?

_____

_____

_____

_____

_____

What happened one time when I took full responsibility for my actions?

_____

_____

_____

_____

_____

How can I take responsibility for something I already made an excuse for?

_____

_____

_____

_____

_____

"Things work out best for those who make the best of how things work out.

~ John Wooden ~

If two people are presented with the same seemingly bad situation, a positive thinker will see an opportunity; a negative, small minded thinker will see failure and think horrible thoughts. Things work out because you make them work. You do this by believing they worked out. Your thoughts are the most controllable choice you have in life. When you make the choice in your mind that things will work out, you exponentially increase the chances that they will work. Even when the worst of the worst happens, as long as you are open to good things, something good will come out of the situation. Candy Lightner is the founder of Mothers Against Drunk Drivers (MADD). She took the terrible situation of her daughter's death and turned that trajectory into something wonderful. If a drunk driver had not killed her daughter, MADD might never have been started, drunk driving laws might still be lenient, and awareness of the dangers of drunk driving may still not be known. MADD has saved an incalculable number of lives. Believe, every time, only good can come from this!

What has been a blessing in disguise?

_____

_____

_____

_____

_____

What past terrible situation can I make the best of now?
How?

_____

_____

_____

_____

_____

How can the worst thing work out for the best?

_____

_____

_____

_____

_____

Since most problems are created by our imagination and are thus imaginary, all we need are imaginary solutions.

~ Richard Bandler ~

What we perceive to be real in our mind is actually 100% false. Our past experiences and thoughts taint our perception of events happening in our lives. A great example of this is during a police investigation. There can be five different witnesses with five different accounts of what happened. Truthfully, if you add up those five witness statements, you may possibly get what actually happened in reality. What we perceive in our minds is our own false reality, it is a world created by your imagination. What matters is what we see and how we perceive it. When you look at life positively, you will see mostly positives. A pessimist can always find negatives in life, even after winning a million dollar lottery. Most of our problems as human beings are a figment of our imagination. To come up with a solution to these "problems", we need to imagine a new way of doing things. Take the challenge to imagine all the good that happens in life, and watch your life transform. You will become happier, healthier and more fulfilled; this is a guarantee.

What problems am I currently producing?

_____

_____

_____

_____

_____

How can I view my present circumstances from a different perspective?

_____

_____

_____

_____

_____

What is the solution I imagined to solve my current problem?

_____

_____

_____

_____

_____

A pessimist sees difficulty in every opportunity. An optimist sees the opportunity in every difficulty.

~ Winston Churchill ~

A pessimist is a negative person who always blames other people, complains about everything, and makes excuses for their actions. An optimist is someone who sees the best in everything and loves life. You can be either one, it is your choice to make. Being an optimist is simply a state of mind. Your thoughts determine whether you are positive or not. All day long, you are presented with opportunities disguised as difficulties. Instead of looking at something as a problem, think of it as an opportunity. Opportunities come in all shapes and sizes when you least expect it, so be prepared. The greatest opportunity comes from a difficult problem which you chose to look at with a positive mind. Difficulties are not excuses to quit. Depending upon your state of mind, you will see difficulties as your time to shine, or as an excuse to quit. They can be difficult to make the most of at times. Remember, everything worthwhile is not easy and everything you are presented with is an opportunity.

How can I make my current problem into an opportunity?

_____

_____

_____

_____

_____

What difficulties was I presented with in the past
which I could have looked at as an opportunity?

_____

_____

_____

_____

_____

How can I maximize my next difficulty and make it an opportunity?

_____

_____

_____

_____

_____

Change your thoughts and you change your world.

~ Norman Vincent Peale ~

Your thoughts make your reality. Everyone does this; do not think you are any different. Your thoughts guide your actions, and your actions produce the results you live. Everything you have in your life, right now, came from your thinking and your thinking alone. All that separates us from each other are our thoughts and actions. On the outside, we are all the same, just another person. What separates the wealthy from the poor are their thought patterns. That is what makes us individuals! They come from years of experience and repetitive phrases getting drilled into us from a young age. You can change your thinking before you even finish reading this sentence; it is your decision to make. Start filling your head with positivity: turn off the TV, stop reading and watching the news. Instead, read self-help books, repeat affirmations, listen to positive audio recordings, and surround yourself with positive people. Figure out who you want to be, determine the thoughts your future self has, and start applying them, today!

What are the three changes I will focus on for the next 18 months?

_____

_____

_____

_____

_____

What thoughts does my future self have on a daily basis?

_____

_____

_____

_____

_____

What thoughts do I need to change to make the above my reality?

_____

_____

_____

_____

_____

We see things not as they are, but as we are.

~ Henry Tomlinson ~

Perception is interpretation! All the experiences we have in life gave us a particular thought process directly affecting how we see and interpret things. For any situation, each participant will have a unique view. Pessimists will find all the bad things. Optimists will see the good and find a way to make it benefit them. Your thought process determines how you see things; it is not reality. No one sees anything as it really is, it is always colored by our past experiences and thoughts. By changing your thoughts to that of a successful person, you will see the best in every situation, not the worst. To be lucky, you must feel lucky, see lucky, and live lucky. Millions of people a year get diagnosed with a life-changing illness; some see how it can benefit themselves and others, while some wallow in despair to the point of death. A positive mind will produce a long, healthy, positive life! The choice is simple and is yours to make.

What has my perception been over the last thirty days?
What would I like it to be over the next thirty days?

_____

_____

_____

_____

_____

What experience(s) from my past do I think about most often?
Why?

_____

_____

_____

_____

_____

What do my current thoughts resemble?
What do I want them to be?

_____

_____

_____

_____

_____

Age is an issue of mind over matter.
If you don't mind, it doesn't matter.

~ Mark Twain ~

Teenagers can accomplish what a seasoned veteran cannot. A senior citizen can accomplish what someone in his or her prime cannot. Age never will matter; the only thing that matters are the thoughts in your mind. There will be some people who look at age as a limitation. Those who are fifteen can accomplish more than someone in their forties. Someone in his or her late nineties can go out and accomplish something that a teenager or middle-aged adult could never do. The saying "mind over matter" is so true. "If you don't mind, it does not matter." You are only as old or as young as you think you are. Age is only a limitation if you let it be. Who is to say what the perfect age is? No one! We all age. The oldest people in the world still learn on a daily basis, so, what is stopping you from achieving greatness? Age has never been, nor will ever be, a valid excuse!

At what age will I be successful?
How did I come up with that conclusion?

_____

_____

_____

_____

_____

How is my age an asset?

_____

_____

_____

_____

_____

What will I tell people who look at my age as a limitation?

_____

_____

_____

_____

_____

It is the mark of an educated mind to be able to entertain a thought without accepting it.

~ Aristotle ~

You do not have to believe everything you hear, nor do you have to accept it. This means that by being a critical thinker, you can think of plausible ways for something to be true, relevant, or worthwhile to understand it. Can you come up with twenty reasons why Adolf Hitler was a great person? Try it! Entertain this notion since he is considered an egomaniacal racist and the worst genocidal mass murderer the world has ever seen. You do not have to accept it, but it is possible for you to come up with more than fifty reasons. This is an important skill to have in life, for it allows you to understand and appreciate other peoples' points of view. You will then be able to easily sympathize with them. Everyone in the world has a different perspective on everything; if you can entertain their opinions without accepting them, you will become a better communicator and be more liked because you will not be pushing your own agenda on everyone else. Your reality is yours, not theirs, so respect other peoples' reality as their own.

Come up with five positive take-a-ways from Adolf Hitler's existence to prove you can entertain any opinionated thought.

_____

_____

_____

_____

_____

How can I remind myself to be more understanding rather than judgmental?

_____

_____

_____

_____

_____

What benefits will I get from asking questions instead of criticizing?

_____

_____

_____

_____

_____

PERCEPTION NOTES

PERCEPTION NOTES

CHAPTER FOUR
ATTITUDE

Attitude: An expression of favor or disfavor toward a person, place, thing, or event (the attitude object). ~ Merriam-Webster

Prominent psychologist Gordon Allport once described attitude as "the most distinctive and indispensable concept in contemporary social psychology." Attitude can be formed from a person's past and present. Attitude is also measurable, changeable, and can influence the person's emotions and behaviors. In lay language, attitude may refer to the distinct concept of mood.

Your demeanor is what people see, it is how you come across as an individual. There are people with good and bad attitudes, positive and negative attitudes. You are labeled by the mindset you have in front of others.

The saying "like attracts like" can be applied to peoples' attitudes. Those with a good, positive approach to life are more attracted to others with like mindset, than to negative individuals expressing bad moods. No positive person enjoys being around negativity. Most negative people feel uncomfortable being around good attitudes. This is life, and this is how we are programmed to operate. If your attitude sucks, you will keep attracting other people with that same attitude into your life.

Your character is a direct reflection of your thoughts. By changing your thoughts, you can change your attitude, and that will change your actions. Changing your actions will change the results you get, and in turn, your life and attitude will change along with it.

"The starting point of all achievement is desire.

~ *Napoleon Hill* ~

There is always a beginning and end to everything you do. To achieve anything, you have to have the desire to achieve what you are working toward. When you have desire, you will have the strength and creativity to overcome the obstacles life will throw at you. In Dr. Stephen Covey's best-selling book *The 7 Habits of Highly Effective People*, his second habit is to "Begin With the End In Mind." Picture what you want to achieve—how it will look, how others will benefit, how you will benefit, etc. Developing this one habit will help develop and strengthen your desire to keep moving forward. The stronger your desire, the more likely it is you will start and finish your dream. If you do not desire to acquire an end result, you will never even begin. In your life right now, you are doing what you desire to do whether you believe it or not. If there is no desire, there will be no action to make it reality. You can believe in yourself all you want, but if it is not backed by desire, the likelihood of starting is nonexistent.

What do I desire to achieve?

_____

_____

_____

_____

_____

What does my end result look, feel, and sound like?
How will it benefit others?

_____

_____

_____

_____

_____

How can I start acting on my desires?
What are my first steps?

_____

_____

_____

_____

_____

Believe you can and you're halfway there.

~ Theodore Roosevelt ~

You will never start something if you do not believe you can do it. Furthermore, you will never start something if you do not suspect you can finish it. The hardest thing to do is to start. To start, you must have confidence in yourself. The second you have that belief, you are halfway there. The major majority of people do not have high expectations for themselves, so they never begin. The only way to begin is to assume you can do something. When you believe you can achieve anything you set your mind to, the hardest part is over. Now it is a simple matter of working at it every day. You are more capable than you think, and you know you can achieve anything you set your mind too. If you need help, ask for it. People love helping other people, but we are all too afraid to ask. Start asking for help; the worst that can happen is they say no. If you have low self-esteem or confidence, start doing tasks that are proven to build these two vital states of mind. Set small goals and celebrate your successes, say affirmations thousands of times a day, eat healthy, exercise, volunteer, get a hobby, write in a journal, read self-help books, and get eight hours of sleep. There are thousands of things you can do to start believing in yourself. Do them even if you are already confident!

What do I want to believe about myself which I currently do not?

_____

_____

_____

_____

_____

What do I believe I am capable of?

_____

_____

_____

_____

_____

How will I build and reinforce the beliefs I have in myself?

_____

_____

_____

_____

_____

If you can dream it, you can achieve it.

~ Zig Ziglar ~

You have the capacity to turn any dream into reality. If it is your dream, it can become your reality. Dream big! The bigger your dreams, the bigger the accomplishment. Too many people have dreams and ideas, but never try to pursue them. Rise above the rest, and stop being average. Your dreams can come true through hard work and perseverance. The hard work part may be why most people never try to pursue their dreams; they would rather help others make their dreams reality by filling out applications and becoming an employee. Your dream may be to work for someone or some company, there is absolutely nothing wrong with that—go out and achieve it. All our dreams are different, and the end results we produce are all original. One person's dream job is the next person's nightmare. Stop listening to other people's opinions—go out and achieve your dreams! Never settle for the easy way out. If you want something, go get it. You are your own biggest obstacle on your journey to achievement. Get past your limiting beliefs and fears of failure. Do what you know you will love!

What dream have I achieved in the past?
How?

_____

_____

_____

_____

_____

What dream am I currently working on achieving?
What are my next steps?

_____

_____

_____

_____

_____

What is the biggest dream I have for my life?
How will I achieve it?

_____

_____

_____

_____

_____

Do not let what you cannot do interfere with what you can do.

~ John Wooden ~

You are not perfect. You cannot do everything, just like others cannot do the things you can do. Everyone is born with gifts and strengths, as well as handicaps and weaknesses. The key is to discover, develop, and use your gifts and strengths while delegating and forgetting about your weaknesses. Not being able to sing, snowboard, sail, or surf does not stop someone from writing a book. Some authors cannot underline all the nouns, verbs, adverbs, or adjectives in a sentence, nor can they properly structure a sentence to please an English teacher. That has not stopped them from writing books or publishing articles. Do not let anyone tell you that you cannot do something because you are not good at it. Artists who have never surfed should not stop themselves from painting a mural of a surfer. You can do so much more than you cannot do. Forget about your handicaps and weaknesses. So you're not a great artist, but you're great with numbers and explaining things. Don't spend your time wishing you could be a better painter. Focus on being better at what you were already born good at. That's where you'll excel in life. Find your abilities and exploit them. Your gifts, talents, and strengths are waiting for you!

What are my core gifts and abilities?
How can I strengthen them?

_____

_____

_____

_____

_____

What do I want to try which I have never tried before?

_____

_____

_____

_____

_____

What are my strengths and talents?
(HINT: Ask family, friends, and StrengthsFinder 2.0)

_____

_____

_____

_____

_____

Life is 10% what happens to us and 90% how we react to it.

~ Charles R. Swindoll ~

We are presented with a multitude of options every day. With each option, we can make only one decision. Each choice closes off many options and opens many more. This cycle repeats endlessly throughout life: situation, options, response. How you respond to the stuff that happens to you opens and closes different paths to your destination. Have you ever thought about something and said, "I would do it differently if I had the chance?" Making decisions based on your values presents millions of options. What life hands you--the situation--is out of your control; how you respond is what is in your control. "Between stimulus and response, there is a space," said Victor Frankl, the psychologist who survived the Nazi death camps. "In that space is our power to choose our response. In that response lies our growth and freedom." How you respond determines your whole life and reality. How you respond is determined by your thoughts. Just because you responded a certain way in the past does not mean you have to keep responding the same way. Everything that happened and your responses brought you to where you are today, right now.

What "reactions" or responses am I proud of which made me who I am?

_____

_____

_____

_____

_____

How can I correct the results of my previous actions
which I am not proud of?

_____

_____

_____

_____

How do I want my life to turn out?
What options do I have to make that happen?

_____

_____

_____

_____

_____

Your problem isn't the problem.
Your reaction is the problem.

~ Anonymous ~

Everyone is presented with problems in life. The trick is to not look at the problem as a problem, but rather as an opportunity. There will always be events in your life that present themselves as problems, if you let them. Your thoughts will determine if it is a problem you cannot overcome, or an opportunity you can use as a stepping-stone to success. When a problem/opportunity is presented, you have millions of choices. How you respond will determine the outcome you receive; nothing more, nothing less. The biggest conflicts people face come from their reactions to life events. If you want the outcome you are looking for, start acting in a way to manifest those desires. The Cuban missile crisis was a problem, and JFK responded carefully, in a way that would bring peace. Had he acted in a different way, we might still be living with the aftereffects of nuclear war. Make the correct choice with your end results in mind.

What "problems" am I currently facing?

_____

_____

_____

_____

_____

How are those "problems" an opportunity?

_____

_____

_____

_____

_____

What is my best course of action?

_____

_____

_____

_____

_____

There are two primary choices in life: to accept conditions as they exist, or accept the responsibility for changing them.

~ *Denis Waitley* ~

Jack Canfield is the co-creator of *Chicken Soup for the Soul*. From 1993–2010 the book sold over 500 million copies in forty-three languages worldwide. In his book *The Success Principles*, he introduces the formula E+R=O (Events + Response = Outcome). You are 100% responsible for your life and the outcomes you produce. You cannot control the (E) events in your life, but you can control your (R) responses to every event that happens. You do this by controlling your thoughts, because inevitably, your thoughts control your actions. Your reaction to an outside factor can give you countless (O) outcomes. Every day, you can take your life in a million different directions by how you respond to all the events that happen. You are the only one who controls your life and the outcomes you live with. Control your reaction, control your outcome!

What areas of life do I need to take responsibility in?

_____

_____

_____

_____

_____

What have I accepted in my life which I am not happy with?

_____

_____

_____

_____

_____

What are the thoughts I should have to live in the conditions I choose?

_____

_____

_____

_____

_____

> # In matters of style,
> # swim with the current;
> # in matters of principle,
> # stand like a rock.

~ Anonymous ~

Over time, the styles of the human race have changed with the whims of the majority, but our morals and values have stood like a rock since the beginning of time. In every country, and every generation, there are different styles that the majority agrees upon as the norm. The styles in Los Angeles are different than the style in New York. In the city of Milwaukee, the style is different on Brady Street versus Milwaukee Street versus Fond du Lac Avenue. When you go with the current, your style is like everyone else, and changes quickly. Good versus bad morals, along with values, are constantly being debated. They do change, but it takes time for the majority to accept changes. When a rock stands still in a river, erosion takes place, wearing the rock down until it is wiped away by the current—accepted by the majority. Think of the erosion process as strikes, sit-ins, and protests. They are not going to get their way instantly, it takes time for critical mass to take hold. Do not get swept away from your principles!

When have I went against my principles and followed the majority?

_____

_____

_____

_____

_____

What principles are my rocks?

_____

_____

_____

_____

_____

How have I gone against who I am just to be accepted?
Why?

_____

_____

_____

_____

_____

A man can be as great as he wants to be. If you believe in yourself and have the courage, the determination, the dedication, the competitive drive and if you are willing to sacrifice the little things in life and pay the price for the things that are worthwhile, it can be done.

~ Vince Lombardi ~

Any and everything is possible, especially with twenty-first century technology! Think of everything we have now that was considered impossible fifty years ago, or even ten years ago. Do not limit yourself based on what society or people around you say about who you are or who you should be. Believe in yourself and everything you are capable of. To pursue any dream, you need to have the courage to face the negativity that will come. You need determination and dedication to keep going after you fail. You need competitive drive to make it better than anyone else could ever dream. You will need to sacrifice time spent on what you normally do, and dedicate it to who you want to become. There will be a price to pay to become the person you want to be, and create something the world sees as worthwhile. Invest in yourself with positive choices, confident in the worthwhile outcome.

How great will I become if I stay on the same path?

_____

_____

_____

_____

_____

How great do I want to become?
(Be specific!)

_____

_____

_____

_____

_____

What am I willing to sacrifice to become great and worthwhile?

_____

_____

_____

_____

_____

Anything I can do, you can do better. It is a matter of belief backed by desire.

~ Lucas J. Robak ~

You can achieve anything you want to achieve, regardless of your disabilities as long as you believe in yourself and have the desire to make it your reality. If you want to be a rocket scientist, but cannot even add, you can still make it happen, as long as you believe you can do it and have the desire to accomplish it. It will be a lot of work, obviously, but it is more than possible. Having a burning desire is not enough, you must first posses the belief in yourself to make it possible. If a rocket scientist wanted to be a rock star, but never held an instrument, it is perfectly possible for that to happen only if they first believe they can do it, then have the desire to sit and practice for hours on end. They may not have the musical talent, but with belief and a burning desire to obtain that rock star status, it is possible. What is easy for one person can be extremely difficult for the next. As long as you believe you can accomplish something, and if you work hard enough, you will be able to do it better than someone with natural talent. Anything and everything can be learned through practice. Believe you can achieve your desires then go out and make it happen.

What do I want to be better at?

_____

_____

_____

_____

What area do I want to known as an expert?

_____

_____

_____

_____

What do I desire most from life?

_____

_____

_____

_____

No one can make you feel inferior without your consent.

~ Eleanor Roosevelt ~

Inferior: Of poor quality: low or lower in quality...of little or less importance or value. ~ Merriam-Webster

Consent: To agree to do or allow something...to give permission for something to happen or be done. ~ Merriam-Webster

Do not allow or give permission to anyone to make you feel low quality, or of less importance. These are your feelings and your life. By choosing to think positively and have feelings of self-worth, you will always be above those who treat you as of little importance. Have a sense of self-worth and treat yourself the way you treat those you love, for you deserve no less. Treat yourself with respect and people will treat you the same. When people talk down to you, and they will, it is up to you to not feel inferior. The feelings you experience are 100% your responsibility; they come from your own thinking. The second someone makes you feel inferior is the second you consented for that to happen. Treat yourself the way you treat your most treasured possessions, and you will live a life of quality.

When was the last time I felt inferior?
How did I allow that to happen?

_____

_____

_____

_____

_____

What are my great qualities which give me worth?
(HINT: Ask friends and family)

_____

_____

_____

_____

_____

How will I react next time someone tries to make me feel inferior?

_____

_____

_____

_____

_____

The mind is everything.
What you think, you become.

~ Buddha ~

Your thoughts dictate your actions. Your actions, accumulated over a period of time, determine what your reality is. If you have thoughts of love and positivity, your actions will follow suit and you will become a respectable human being who people admire. If you have thoughts of fear and negativity, likewise, your actions will follow suit and you will become lonely and despised by others. You can control your thoughts by thinking about thinking. Be conscious of your thoughts, and in time, it will become habit to think thoughts of abundance, or whatever it is that you choose. Determine who you want to become, and research the thoughts those kinds of people have. Make those thoughts your core focus until they are habit! Become the person you want to become simply by thinking. Indeed, thoughts are things!

Who do I want to become?

_____

_____

_____

_____

_____

What thoughts do I need to eliminate from my mind?

_____

_____

_____

_____

_____

What thoughts do I need to have?

_____

_____

_____

_____

_____

ATTITUDE NOTES

ATTITUDE NOTES

CHAPTER FIVE
FEAR

Fear is only a state of mind. It is the result of limiting thoughts. Fear goes away with practice and constant repetition. The repetition can be in the form of thoughts or actions. If something scares you to think about, by doing that fearful action, you will overcome your fear, and may actually come to love doing it.

Think back to when you were little and saw a diving board the first time. You watched everyone else having fun jumping off it. When you got on the diving board and saw how high off the water the low dive actually was, you may have gotten scared and wimped out. You might have taken your time to jump in feet first, as close to the wall as possible, for a quick escape. Whatever you did, eventually, after a few more times off of the board, you were no longer afraid of it. Your thoughts changed. In time, you may have been doing dives, flips, or even back-flips off of the board.

Fear is what lies outside of our comfort zone. Our comfort zone is what will always keep our lives stagnant. If we do not face our fears and live out of our comfort zone, we will always be in the same place and never make any advancement in life. Remember that accomplishments will always be achieved outside your comfort zone. Living a life without facing your fears is a life no one will ever remember. You won't want to even remember it!

You can run from your problems but not from the flaws in your thinking. Always start by fixing your brain. Train it to remove logical fallacies.

~ Tai Lopez ~

You have a perception of the world, it is yours and yours alone. Your internal image of your problems will be impossible to overcome until you change your thinking. This is as easy as making the choice to change your thinking, or as hard as living your whole life and realizing on your deathbed that it was not difficult at all. A real difficulty is only as hard as you make it. If you think everything is easy, it will be. The hardest of tasks can be broken down into a lot of action steps so they are not as difficult. It is as simple as that. A real difficulty will take more thinking, time, and action steps over something easy. The only thing holding you back is your limiting beliefs about yourself and all the fallacies you were raised to believe. Your imagination can be your worst enemy or your greatest asset. Stop turning your thoughts against yourself and conquer your dreams!

What have I given up on because of the false limiting beliefs
my parents, teachers, coaches, and friends projected upon me?

_____

_____

_____

_____

_____

What imaginary difficulties do I face on a daily basis?

_____

_____

_____

_____

_____

How can I overcome my current difficult situation?

_____

_____

_____

_____

_____

Too many of us are not living our dreams because we are living our fears.

~ Les Brown ~

Fear is the root of all failure. Fear is what stops us from trying or moving forward in difficult times. We live in fear on a day-to-day basis. Instead of moving toward our goals, we move away from our fears. It is a catch-22, because our goals lie deep within our fears. To accomplish any worthwhile goal, you have to face your fears and step out of your comfort zone. There is a way around never facing your fears: never set any goals, live an unaccomplished life, allow circumstances and other people to control every aspect of your life, and be miserable. —OR— Place your fears in front of you, defeat them by facing them, and thrive within them. For every fear you have, there are millions of people who live with it every day. Those same people have their own fears which millions of others live with. Fear is a state of mind which you can overcome through repetition. Constantly face your fears, and they will no longer keep you from living your dreams!

What fears am I living in?

_____

_____

_____

_____

_____

What fears do I need to get over in order for me to live my dreams?

_____

_____

_____

_____

_____

What can I realistically do to ease myself
into being comfortable with my fears?

_____

_____

_____

_____

_____

When one door of happiness closes, another opens, but often we look so long at the closed door that we do not see the one that has been opened for us.

~ Helen Keller ~

The past is the past; get over it and move on. Too often we dwell on the past when we lose something or someone, and that blinds us to all the opportunities that continue to appear. Time will move on, with or without us. No matter how good or bad we feel, the sun will still rise tomorrow. "For every door that closes, one more opens" is a potent truth. Truly believe that for every door that closes, an entire floor of doors open. Opportunities and choices are endless. Once one door closes, you no longer have that possibility blinding you from seeing what is behind the next ten thousand doors. When a door closes on you, that moment is your opportunity. You can look at the door, but do not have to walk through it. Meaning, be open to and see what opportunities are out there for you. Choose the ones you want.

What opportunities do I have available to me right now?

_____

_____

_____

_____

_____

What are the greatest benefits I will receive from
going through that newly opened door?

_____

_____

_____

_____

_____

What opportunities do I want available to me in the near future?
How will I create them?

_____

_____

_____

_____

_____

I am always doing that which I cannot do, in order that I may learn how to do it.

~ Pablo Picasso ~

No matter what the field, even the most talented people did not know how to do it at one point. Computer programmers could not program anything until they learned how. A great leader did not just pop up from out of nowhere, they learned how to do what they do. You can learn anything and everything you want to. The only thing holding you back is you. There are many options when it comes to learning something new. You can teach yourself through reading, YouTube, and most importantly by doing it. You can learn from those who have already accomplished what you want to learn, through lessons, seminars, workshops, and books. You can learn more by doing than you ever would by sitting in a classroom for decades. True mastery comes from practice, not from being lectured. You cannot learn how to play a guitar by studying music, you learn by playing the instrument. You do not need knowledge to do things, you simply need to start doing it!

What have I learned from doing?
(Not walking, talking, reading, the bathroom, and using a cell phone)

_____

_____

_____

_____

_____

What do I want to learn to do?
(List everything that comes to mind)

_____

_____

_____

_____

_____

How am I able to learn what I want to learn?
What do I need to do to acquire this knowledge?

_____

_____

_____

_____

_____

Don't let the fear of losing be greater than the excitement of winning.

~ Robert Kiyosaki ~

Most people develop the fear of losing, and lose sight of what can be gained. When a sports team takes the field, they are excited about the win and what that will bring, rather than not showing up because they fear losing. Taking risks is scary because of the fear of losing everything. The reason people do risk everything is because of what will be gained when they succeed. This creates billionaires, they risk everything they have and come out on top, usually after numerous attempts and bankruptcies. Robert Kiyosaki is a self-made billionaire and owner of *Rich Dad Education* who at one point lived out of his car. The fear of losing should never hold you back. Start thinking in terms of what can be gained, and you will succeed. It will give you courage and perseverance to get through all the tough times which lie ahead.

What could I lose by taking that risk I am thinking of?

_____

_____

_____

_____

_____

What will I gain from taking that risk?

_____

_____

_____

_____

_____

How will my life be different after winning?

_____

_____

_____

_____

_____

Dream big and dare to fail.

~ Norman Vaughan ~

The bigger the dream, the bigger the reward. The bigger the reward, the bigger the risk. The bigger the risk, the bigger the fear. When you have a big dream, there is a great chance you will fail—big. Do not let the fear of failure stop you from working toward making your dream a reality. The only way to accomplish anything is by daring failure to stop you. The only way you will fail is the second you decide to give up completely. You may decide one day to give up and the next day to start again; that is not failure because you are still working toward your dream. Dare to fail, and you will succeed. Believe in yourself and have the desire to achieve, and there will be nothing that can stop you. When you have a dream, an idea, you have that for a reason. It is up to you to make it into reality. Stop thinking someone else will do it; you are that someone else. Face fear and failure head on to achieve your wildest dreams!

What are all of my big dreams?

_____

_____

_____

_____

_____

What is my biggest dream?

_____

_____

_____

_____

_____

What positive outcome can come from accomplishing my biggest dream?

_____

_____

_____

_____

_____

"All progress takes place outside the comfort zone.

~ Michael John Bobak ~

Your comfort zone is a very small box which only you live in. However, many people are in this small box of a comfort zone and each person is just as lonely as the next. It is a lonely, over crowded place which allows zero growth. You will constantly be living the same life situations and getting the same results until you step outside of it. When something scares you, do it. When something is outside your comfort zone, do it. Fear is essential to growth and for creating new opportunities. You develop new skills and meet new people when you leave your comfort zone behind. The current life that you have is comfortable to you, but if you stayed there for the rest of your life, would you be satisfied? No, you would potentially feel unfulfilled living the exact same life for decades with zero growth. The only way to make progress in your life is to step outside your comfort zone, face your fears, and make things happen for yourself.

How is my comfort zone limiting me?

_____

_____

_____

_____

_____

What do I want to do which is outside my comfort zone?

_____

_____

_____

_____

_____

What excitement will I experience by doing something that scares me?

_____

_____

_____

_____

_____

No man ever achieved worth-while success who did not, at one time or other, find himself with at least one foot hanging well over the bring of failure.

~ *Napoleon Hill* ~

To succeed, your desire for the outcome must be stronger than your fears. You might fear failure, success, big crowds, or public speaking. In order to be accomplished, you have to get out of your comfort zone and make things happen. Nothing will ever happen in your comfort zone. Success is what people in their comfort zones watch others have. Courage is grace under pressure of fear; fear remains, it is just the ability to face it. Stop being afraid of things that other people are not afraid of. Make it a point each day to face one of your fears. If you are human, you have a whole list of fears. If something scares you or makes you uncomfortable to think about, do not hesitate, do it!

What's one fear I will need to face?

_____

_____

_____

_____

_____

What can I do to live outside my comfort zone once a day?

_____

_____

_____

_____

_____

What do I need to do to succeed which elicits fear
by simply thinking about it?

_____

_____

_____

_____

_____

FEAR NOTES

FEAR NOTES

CHAPTER SIX
FAILURE

We are more likely to see successful people when they are at the top, rather than seeing all the failures along the way. In the end, you will fail more times than you will succeed. Today, begin to see failure from a different perspective. See everything as an experiment. Experiments are a way to learn and receive feedback so that you can make changes and do it better the next time you try.

Do not blame your parents or teachers; they all do the best they can with what they have. Simply accept responsibility for making the necessary changes in your life.

It is time to start thinking like a successful person as soon as you can, look at failing as opportunity, a learning process, an experiment. The only time you will get a grade lower than an "A" is when you quit because you did not succeed the first few thousand times. Failing only comes from giving up.

Embrace failure, because it is the only way you will become a success. So many people give up before they even try because they fear failure. Other people give up after failing their first time. Not many people make it past that. The more you embrace your failures, the better chance you give yourself at success.

The road to success and the road to failure are almost exactly the same.

~ Colin R. Davis ~

In life, you can take any road you want and still make it to where you want to go. You can do this by turning around, cutting across fields, or sticking it out to see what happens. The only way you can make any of these diversions to become your road to success is to keep truckin' past all the roadblocks, accidents, and checkpoints. That is the only way you will succeed. The same road many people are on has potential to lead each vehicle to a different destination. When you come to intersections and bypasses—your daily choices—you can go in millions of directions. There will be times when it appears you are headed in the wrong direction because of the failures you encounter, but by staying on that same road, all those failures will take you to your destination of success.

When did I think I was failing, but then succeeded?

_____

_____

_____

_____

What direction have I decided to take as my life's destination?

_____

_____

_____

_____

What is the worst that can happen when I persevere through my failures?

_____

_____

_____

_____

Many of life's failures are experienced by people who did not realize how close they were to success when they gave up.

~ Thomas Edison ~

People give up far too easily. Many give up just before success takes hold. Success is always one more try away. If you keep giving it one more try, you will succeed. It is a universal law! Success comes to those who do not quit. It is hard for someone to fail if they never give up. You will never know how close you are to success until you become a success. Failure is giving up, quitting. You will never be a success if you stop trying when it could have been one more try away. Also, look at who said this quote—Thomas Edison. It took Thomas Edison ten thousand tries to make a light bulb. We would still be living with oil lamps and candles if he had given up at try 9,999. He experimented ten thousand times, and changed the world.

What did I give up on before I succeeded?

_____

_____

_____

_____

_____

What would my world be like if I kept trying until I succeeded?

_____

_____

_____

_____

_____

What should I give 10,000 more tries at success?

_____

_____

_____

_____

_____

Develop success from failures. Discouragement and failure are two of the surest stepping stones to success.

~ Dale Carnegie ~

You will fail! This is a guarantee in life; there is no way around it other than to never try at all. Each failure you encounter opens up more opportunities and is a great learning experience. Learn what you did right, what you did wrong, and how you can do it differently the next time around. When you do it again, take note of what went right and what went wrong, whether or not you succeeded. There is huge potential in learning from your successes. You will never do something with absolute perfection, there will always be room for improvement. When you fail, you may experience symptoms such as dismay, depression, moping around, pessimism, and you end up giving up. These feelings are a part of the natural process on your journey to success, anyone worth mentioning went through it at some point many times. Keep experimenting, and you will succeed.

What was my greatest failure?
What did I learn?

_____

_____

_____

_____

_____

What made me experience one, or all, of the symptoms of failure?

_____

_____

_____

_____

_____

What did I learn from my failures?
How can I do it differently next time?

_____

_____

_____

_____

_____

An obstacle is often a stepping-stone.

~ William Prescott ~

When you climb stairs, each step helps you get to the next one. All are necessary to get to the top. Every hardship in your life will help you grow and take you to the next obstacle. Add up all the difficulties, build a staircase with them, and get to where you are going. Hurdles are a necessary part of the process by helping you develop the skills necessary to build you as a person. All the stairs you climb help build your muscles so you can keep climbing every staircase you want. Doing stair exercises is a great workout and helps you stay in shape, the same goes for obstacles. Every bump makes you stronger and helps you get closer to your destination. They are a great way to learn new skills, meet new people, and face your fears so you grow as an individual. If there were no obstacles, this would be a perfect world and everyone would get what they wanted. Thankfully, that is not the case; you have to work for what you want, and persist through the hard times. Life is never easy, and it never will be. However, it is easy to get jealous and demand you have the right to other people's success; it is hard to go out and become a success yourself. Get past the stumbling blocks and succeed in life.

What obstacles helped put me in the
direction of something better?

_____

_____

_____

_____

_____

What learning came from my obstacles?

_____

_____

_____

_____

_____

What skills have I developed because of an obstacle?

_____

_____

_____

_____

_____

A person who never made a mistake never tried anything new.

~ Albert Einstein ~

The only way to learn something new is through making mistakes. Even if you did all your homework and acquired all the knowledge you need, miscalculations will still be made. When you actually do something, you learn more in that one attempt than from decades of studying, reading, and being in a classroom. You will make mistakes, and you probably will fail more times than you would like. That is a part of the learning process. Learn by doing! Learn by failing! Learn by making mistakes! Learn through risk taking! Learn through repetition! Get off your butt and make as many mistakes as you possibly can, learn from them, then get out there and do it again differently with your new knowledge. Continue this process tens of thousands of times until you produce the results you want.

What new things have I tried recently?
What did I learn from my mistakes?

What new things am I thinking about trying?
What am I waiting for?

What mistakes will I make in the future?
What can I do to avoid them?

" Every strike brings me closer to the next home run.

~ Babe Ruth ~

In his career, Babe Ruth had 714 home runs and struck out 1,330 times. Each strikeout means he saw three pitches, minimum, each time he was at bat. So Babe Ruth saw, at minimum, 3,990 strikes thrown at him in order to hit those 714 home runs; that's an 18% success rate. If each strike is seen by Babe Ruth as a failure, and each home run a success, he failed over five-and-a-half times more than he succeeded. In life, most people do not even attempt to go to the plate out of fear of failure, and never see one pitch. To truly succeed, you will have to fail more times than you succeed. The public does not see the failures, they see the success that may take decades to manifest into reality. All those failures will make you into a successful person! True winners are the ones who make the most errors. We remember Babe Ruth as a baseball legend, not the strike-out king.

In the past, how many times did I fail before I succeeded?

_____

_____

_____

_____

_____

What is my most recent "strike"
which brought me closer to my next "home run"?

_____

_____

_____

_____

_____

What am I trying to achieve this week/month/year/decade?

_____

_____

_____

_____

_____

FAILURE NOTES

FAILURE NOTES

CHAPTER SEVEN
DREAMS

Dream: To contemplate the possibility of doing something or that something might be the case. ~ Merriam-Webster

Dreams come in many forms to inspire you to successful action and determination. Dreams and visions might come in your sleep as an actual dream, or while you are awake, through ideas, hunches, feelings, and guidance. They are not limited to that; everyone is different, just like all of our dreams.

A dream's worst nightmare is a dream stealer or dream killer. These are people who try to crush your dream, or get you to give up on it. They can be your parents, teachers, family, friends, neighbors, coaches, and strangers. Dream stealers are everywhere you turn. You will learn that you may want to keep your dreams to yourself, because a dream stealer will do anything they can to make you give up.

People become dream stealers because they do not believe in themselves enough to achieve their own objectives. They will tell you all sorts of bogus phrases such as, "You can't do that," "That's impossible," "That's stupid," or "You're not smart enough." You could easily make your own list of negative phrases you've heard from these awful people.

Your dreams are yours; they came into your head for a reason. It is up to you to create the life you dream of.

Great minds discuss ideas.
Average minds discuss events.
Small minds discuss people.

~ Henry Thomas Buckle ~

Think about the people who surround you. You are the average of the five people you hang out with most. What do you talk about? Ideas turn into reality; events are things of the past; people are not worth discussing, because gossip has no value. When you hear people talk about ideas and all the possibilities life has to offer, it is exciting, even for those who just listen in. When people talk about events of the past, they are talking about something they cannot control, and no longer matters. When you talk about people, it is usually complaining about them—pure negativity. When you discuss ideas, you are inspiring yourself and others. Look around right now and notice what is around you. Everything you see started out as a dream. If it wasn't for someone turning his or her idea into reality, you would have nothing in your life but wilderness. Become that great thinker you were meant to be by surrounding yourself with big thinkers and isolating the small-minded dream stealers of your life.

What do I find myself normally discussing?
How do I feel after those conversations?

_____

_____

_____

_____

_____

What is one statement or question I can ask to turn a small-minded or
average conversation into one that great minds have?

_____

_____

_____

_____

_____

What are five things I can do to start having conversations
about ideas more often?

_____

_____

_____

_____

_____

Great spirits have always encountered violent opposition from mediocre minds.

~ Albert Einstein ~

Immediately after the above, Einstein wrote in his letter to Morris Raphael Cohen, "The mediocre mind is incapable of understanding the man who refuses to bow blindly to conventional prejudices and chooses instead to express his opinions courageously and honestly." When you have a new idea, you will encounter conflict from small-minded thinkers who are set in their ways; these same small-minded people will be the first to say, "have an open mind" or "think out of the box". Once you are able to deal with conflict confidently, tactfully and maturely, you can get past all of life's negativity. You may even win some negative people to your side. When people do not agree with you, their words, and sometimes their actions, become violent so as to silence you and make you give up. Learn how to deal with conflict, and you will succeed!

How do I currently deal with conflict?
How has it been working for me?

_____

_____

_____

_____

_____

What have I given up because of conflict
with a mediocre, average, or small mind?

_____

_____

_____

_____

_____

What are my options to avoid the small, mediocre minds of my life?

_____

_____

_____

_____

_____

The person who says it cannot be done should not interrupt the person who is doing it.

~ Chinese Proverb ~

A dream stealer is someone who gave up on his or her dreams, and wants to get you to give up on yours. They are the ones who tried, failed, and gave up. In their minds it cannot be done, so they want everyone who is still trying to know that it is impossible. A dream stealer is someone who does not have any critical thinking skills; they are small thinkers. These small-minded people do not see the big picture of what could be. Rather, they see all the things that could go wrong, and all the reasons why one should not even try. A small-minded person does not believe in himself or herself enough to believe in anyone else. They are the ones who gave up and put themselves on the sidelines to watch everyone else succeed, while they boo, taunt, and try to bring everyone else down. Unless a dream stealer's effort inspires you to succeed, these people are irrelevant, and you need to ignore their attempts to steal your dream. You may even kick them completely out of your life if you want.

What did I accomplish after
a dream stealer told me it could not be done?

_____

_____

_____

_____

_____

What am I working on that I was told was impossible?

_____

_____

_____

_____

_____

What is something that I believe to be impossible,
but is something I want to accomplish?

_____

_____

_____

_____

_____

There are two types of people who will tell you that you cannot make a difference in this world: those who are afraid to try themselves, and those who are afraid you will succeed.

~ Ray Goforth ~

Many call them dream stealers. You will encounter dream stealers at every turn in life, from the day you are born until the day you die. The most important thing to remember is that these people and their opinions are completely irrelevant to you and your dreams. They chose to develop the victim mindset because they too encountered others who stole their dreams. They were too afraid to try or try again, and they gave up. They will tell you it is impossible or stupid. They may be filled with jealousy, envy, and bitterness. Unconsciously, they do not want people to succeed because they want to keep others at their level. Small minds, negative people, and dream stealers bring people down; winners help others succeed and are happy when they do. Look for the winners in life. When you come across a dream stealer—and you will—remember: their opinions are irrelevant to your passions and purpose.

Who are the dream stealers in my life?

_____

_____

_____

_____

_____

What dreams have I given up on because of a dream stealer?

_____

_____

_____

_____

_____

What dreams do I want to pursue again?
How will I steal back my dreams and ignore the dream stealers?

_____

_____

_____

_____

_____

The number one reason people fail in life is because they listen to their friends, family, and neighbors.

~ Napoleon Hill ~

Beginning in childhood, we are told what to do, what to think, and how to act. Who we are today is a result of the environments we grew up in. If you take a child born in Milwaukee, Wisconsin, and raise it in Nanjin, China, the chance of that child being able to speak English is small. As we get older, the people in our lives can still determine what we become, because we allow it to happen. Your family, friends, teachers, coaches, and neighbors are the people most able to discourage you from pursuing your dreams. But only if you allow it. If you share an idea you have with one of them, they may try to talk you out of it because it is not their dream for themselves or for you, or because they do not believe in themselves. You are your own person, and you have the potential to achieve anything you want in life. Stop listening to other people, and start listening to yourself!

What goal has the negativity of my friends, family,
teachers, and/or neighbors held me back from?

_____

_____

_____

_____

_____

In what areas of my life do I need to stop listening to these people?

_____

_____

_____

_____

_____

Who do I need to kick out of my life because of their negativity?
How will I tactfully do it?

_____

_____

_____

_____

_____

There is only one way to avoid criticism: do nothing, say nothing, and be nothing.

~ Elbert Hubbarb ~

There are always trolls out there who will criticize what you do and/or how you do it. The only way to avoid criticism is to never try. Those with ideas and dreams are often the ones who get criticized the most. When you do nothing, you will accomplish nothing. When you say nothing, you will not be heard, and you allow other people to control your circumstances. Doing nothing brings nothing. When someone criticizes you, it is feedback you are doing something right. You will never be able to please everyone, and if you do, you are definitely doing something wrong. When you receive criticism, turn it into constructive criticism because you are on the right path for yourself!

What criticism do I regularly receive?
How can I make it constructive to my goals?

_____

_____

_____

_____

_____

What criticism am I actively avoiding?
What harm is that doing?

_____

_____

_____

_____

_____

What is the best that can happen for me when I stop avoiding
and give up my fear of criticism?

_____

_____

_____

_____

_____

Whatever the mind can conceive and believe, the mind can achieve.

~ Napoleon Hill ~

This quote is written numerous times throughout Napoleon Hill's best-selling book, *Think and Grow Rich*. If you have not already, Read that book! The book is a collection of wisdom garnered from studying the lives and behavior of extremely successful people for twenty years. Published in 1937, the classic book reveals this universal truth, which he observed in all successful people. Whatever idea your mind can come up with, as long as you believe it possible, you will be able to make it a reality. This does not mean it will be an easy process, or that your idea will be reality within a day or even a decade. It means you have the power to create anything your mind imagines. Everything we have today all started out as a simple idea, backed by years of hard work, determination, and perseverance. Your dreams, ideas, and imagination are your most valuable assets; treat them as such. Believe in yourself, and you will accomplish unbelievably incredible dreams. Millions who started out just like you already have, and you can, too.

What ideas do I have which I would like to see become reality?

_____

_____

_____

_____

_____

What do I believe I can possibly achieve in this lifetime?

_____

_____

_____

_____

_____

What would I like to achieve but do not believe I can at this moment?

_____

_____

_____

_____

_____

DREAMS NOTES

DREAMS NOTES

CHAPTER EIGHT
GOALS

Goals are important to many people and organizations today. Some people do not like to set goals for themselves, preferring to focus on taking a journey rather than working towards a definite outcome. Whichever path feels right for you, know that this section is about creating the results you choose. If you do not like to use the word goal, use some other term such as: outcome, results, objective, target, design, destination, end, mission, mark, duty, intention, evidence, etc. In this section, the term "goal" is used, but if you are not comfortable with that word, replace it with a more empowering term.

If you are achieving 100% of your goals 100% of the time, they are way too small. Adjust your goals higher to stretch yourself. If you are achieving less than 90% of your goals, they are too big. Adjust your goals lower to maintain confidence and momentum.

"You measure the size of the accomplishment by the obstacles you had to overcome to reach your goals.

~ Booker T. Washington ~

Creating a goal and succeeding is not about what you gain from the results, but rather who you become along the way. It is what you learn, the skills you acquire, the obstacles you overcome, and who you become as a person. The tougher the obstacles, the bigger the accomplishments. Think in terms of traveling. One goal is to walk to the grocery store and back. The obstacles you might face are stairs, doors, traffic, traffic lights, people, and a line. Another goal is to get to the other side of the country, with no money, within three days. Think of those obstacles you will have to overcome. The level of difficulty in the task will directly affect your satisfaction and feeling of accomplishment. Granted, not everyone can walk to the grocery store, and some people may consider that as one of their biggest accomplishments. Everyone is different in their own deserving right.

What are the biggest obstacles I am currently facing?

_____

_____

_____

_____

_____

What accomplishment do I need to achieve so I can say,
"This is the biggest accomplishment of my life?"

_____

_____

_____

_____

_____

What will happen if I don't get it?
What won't happen if I do get it?

_____

_____

_____

_____

_____

The successful warrior is the average man, with laser-like focus.

~ Bruce Lee ~

We are all one in the same. The only thing that separates us from each other is our thoughts. Focus falls into this category. To have laser-like focus is to ignore all distractions around us. Technically speaking, we are all average people, some more focused than others. Focus comes from desire and passion to finish a task or project. Whether assigned or started on your own, it is the passion and desire that gives you the focus you need to ignore all distractions and successfully complete the task. As people, we all have the same decision to make, choose to create a bunch of lame excuses and reasons to cry out on the mountain top, or we can choose to produce results. What's better, creating reasons or creating results?

What do I do which gives me the most focus?

_____

_____

_____

_____

_____

What distractions can I eliminate when working
on accomplishing something?
(HINT: Technology)

_____

_____

_____

_____

_____

What time of day do I get the most work done?

_____

_____

_____

_____

_____

To accomplish great things;
we must not only act, but also dream;
not only plan, but also believe.

~ Anatole France ~

All achievements begin as an idea from one's imagination. Whether it is from the creative imagination (completely original) or the synthetic imagination (using what has already been created to make something new), all accomplishments start out as just a dream, an idea, a vision. Motivation comes from the daily belief in oneself to be able to manifest the idea. A great plan or goal does not need to be detailed or elaborate. Goals and plans change as you learn. The only way to learn is to start acting on your plan, your dream. Through the simple act of doing, taking action, you will open up more opportunities and learn more than just simply reading a book and listening to a lecture. Get out there and make it happen!

What is a dream I have for myself?

_____

_____

_____

_____

_____

What will happen when I get it?

_____

_____

_____

_____

What resources will I use to get it?

_____

_____

_____

_____

If you don't design your own life plan, chances are you'll fall into someone else's plan. And guess what they have planned for you? Not much.

~ Jim Rohn ~

If you do not know where you are going, you will not know which way to turn or even when you arrive. When you drive to school or work, you know where you are starting from and where your destination is. On your way there, you know when and where to turn. You are even able to take different routes if there is an accident or a traffic jam. Also, you clearly know when you arrive. However, if you are falling into someone else's plan, who has nothing planned for you, you may not even be able to find your car. That "someone else" took your car because you going to where you needed to be was not a part of their plan. There are a lot of bosses out there who only think about themselves and their goals because they are the ones paying you to create their dream, not your dream. If you getting to work was not a part of that plan, there is nothing to stop them from taking your car. This is why goals for yourself is so important. Take control of your life and make a plan for where you want to go! Chances are, people will bend over backwards to help you along the way!

What plan am I a part of that is not mine?
How can I change that?

_____

_____

_____

_____

_____

What is the life I want to live?
What plan do I need to implement for it happen?

_____

_____

_____

_____

_____

What resources do I currently have which will assist me?
What resources do I need to acquire?

_____

_____

_____

_____

_____

The reason most people never reach their goals is that they don't define them, or ever seriously consider them as believable or achievable. Winners can tell you where they are going, what they plan to do along the way, and who will be sharing the adventure with them.

~ Denis Waitley ~

When setting a goal, use the NLP SMART Goal technique. Refer back to page 146.

(S) is a balance between **S**pecific and **S**imple. Make it easy enough for a 5-year-old child to tell others and to let you know how close you are to achieving it if you haven't already.

(M) is to make it **M**eaningful to you. Pursuing this has to be your choice which supports your purpose.

(A) has two meanings: the goal should address **A**ll **A**reas of your life, and be written **A**s if it is your current reality. With anything in life, your goals should ideally be in harmony with your values, principles, and the six areas of life (Career/School, Health & Fitness, Relationships, Family, Personal Development, and Spiritual Growth).

(R) is to determine if the goal is **R**esponsible and Ecological. Think about the consequences, both good and bad, of achieving your goal for yourself and the world around you.

(T) is to make sure you are going **T**oward what you want by a certain **T**ime. When setting a deadline, it is always a guess!

LOOK AT MY NLP SMART GOAL!

S

Specifically Simple:
What is my specific and simple goal?
How is it measurable?

M

Meaningful:
What does obtaining this goal mean for me?
For what purpose do I want it?

A

All Areas of your life, written As if is a reality now:
What areas of my life are impacted
by the achievement of this goal?

R

Responsible & Ecological:
What are the consequences, both good and bad,
of achieving the goal for myself and the world?

T

Toward what you want by what Time:
By when will this goal be completed?
Verify you're moving towards, not away from something.

_____

_____

_____

_____

_____

_____

_____

_____

_____

_____

The trouble with not having a goal is that you can spend your life running up and down the field and never score.

~ Bill Copeland ~

A goal is a destination. In basketball it is the hoop; in soccer, hockey, lacrosse, etc. it is the net; football and rugby it is the end zone. Athletes know exactly where they need to end up to win. Life is the same way. If you do not have a goal, how will you know you achieved anything? When you do not know where you are going—in sports, driving, life in general—you will aim mindlessly and never actually know if you succeeded. Have a goal and know where you are going! It boosts self-esteem and gives your life direction.

What are five outcomes I want to achieve?
What is my start and finish date?

What are five outcomes I want to achieve in the next ninety days?
What is my start and finish date?

What will not happen if I achieve this?
How will my life change when I achieve this?

GOALS NOTES

GOALS NOTES

CHAPTER NINE
ACTION

If you remember back to *Schoolhouse Rock*, they made the bold claim that knowledge is power. Knowledge is not power!

Knowledge is simply perceived power.
Action, and action alone, is true power.

There are people who are considered geniuses, but do absolutely nothing with their life and the knowledge they acquire. When you gather knowledge, you gather knowledge, and that is all. Action alone is where the magic happens, even if you have zero knowledge with what you're acting upon.

When was the last time you read a finance book and instantly had a million dollars in your bank account? You need to take action in order to create anything in life, not just with finances. When you act on your dreams and ideas, that is when you start making things happen in order to turn them into reality.

You can have the highest I.Q. in the world and be flipping burgers at McDonald's because you never took action on what you knew. The best part is that you do not need to know everything before you begin. If you think you have to know everything first, you will never begin; there is so much information out there that you could always be learning, and never doing.

Take action today.

Now!

All our dreams can come true— if we have the courage to pursue them.

~ Walt Disney ~

The number one thing that holds most people back from starting anything is fear. Fear of failure, fear of success, fear of ridicule, and so on. Believe that you can live the life you dream of. Everything starts out as just a dream, and we can benefit from other people's courage to overcome the obstacles life throws at us. Courage is nothing more than looking at failure as feedback, rather than a reason to give up and let someone else achieve your dream! Courage is a state of mind that you can develop over time. Walt Disney was fired from a job because he was told he had no imagination. That did not stop him from taking action and creating a global empire.

Which of my dreams have I not pursued, yet?

_____

_____

_____

_____

_____

How will the community benefit from the completion of my dream?

_____

_____

_____

_____

_____

Who do I need to look to for the courage to proceed?

_____

_____

_____

_____

_____

Vision without action is a daydream. Action without vision is a nightmare.

~ Japanese Proverb ~

Everything we have in life started out as an idea, a vision. We all have them every day. The only way to turn your vision into reality is through action and perseverance. If you do not act on your ideas, they will never manifest themselves. "No one will do your push-ups for you." The opposite end of the spectrum is acting when you have no vision. This is not a good thing either because if you have no vision, goal, or end in mind, you have no direction. When you do not have direction, you will not know what to do next, or even why you are doing something. A vision, coupled with action, is essential to success. With no action, your dream will never be a reality. With no vision, you go through the motions without direction.

What happened when I started doing something
before thinking about how to accomplish it?

_____

_____

_____

_____

_____

What vision have I yet to take action on?

_____

_____

_____

_____

_____

What are my first action steps to make my vision a reality?

_____

_____

_____

_____

_____

The journey of a thousand miles begins with one step.

~ Lao Tzu ~

Everything starts somewhere. You cannot start a project from the middle. There will always be a beginning, middle, and end. When you go on a road trip, it starts even before you pack your bags: you make plans. When you begin driving, you have a starting point. Think of a big goal laid out before you as a trip of a thousand miles. For each mile in that journey, there are thousands of steps you need to take. You cannot take those steps until you start. You do not need to know all the directions and all the steps before you start; all you need to do is start. How you start really is not that big of a deal. As long as you start, you will begin to see what you should do to put yourself on the right path. Start! Take action today!

What is one desire that I want to be reality?

_____

_____

_____

_____

_____

What do I think are my first few steps?

_____

_____

_____

_____

_____

What will I regret if I do not take these first steps?

_____

_____

_____

_____

_____

The best time to plant a tree was twenty years ago. The second best time is now.

~ Chinese Proverb ~

All you have is your immediate present to do something. If you used your immediate present a year ago to take action, your life would be drastically different than it is now. Do not dwell on the past! Do not regret not having done something because that will inhibit you from moving forward. Take action now: your immediate present is the only time you will ever have to change your life. Nothing will happen without you taking action in your present moment. Make up for lost time, and use everything you learned over the course of your inaction to be successful now. If you passed up an opportunity before, do not dwell on it. Instead, create that opportunity again. Make it happen. Reap the benefits, and live it up!

What did I not start before which I wish I had?

_____

_____

_____

_____

_____

What are the benefits I would be receiving if I had taken action?

_____

_____

_____

_____

_____

What can I do now to take action so that I will live those benefits?

_____

_____

_____

_____

_____

" It is never too late to be what you might have been.

~ George Eliot ~

If you had followed through on something you gave up on, you would already be living the benefits. Do not get discouraged, the great thing about life is that it is never too late to start again. Even if you are in your eighties, you can achieve the life you wanted when you were in your twenties. Some limitations apply, but that should not stop you. The only time you fail is when you give up completely. It may take decades to come back to your original plan, but this is your second chance. Achieve the life you've always wanted!

What dream have I given up on but is still in my mind?

_____

_____

_____

_____

_____

What does the final outcome look, feel, and sound like?

_____

_____

_____

_____

_____

What are the first three action steps I will take this week?

_____

_____

_____

_____

_____

Good things come to people who wait, but better things come to those who go out and get them.

~ Anonymous ~

Patience is a virtue, but what is even better is taking the initiative. If you sit and wait around for something great to happen to you, the chances are not good. If you go out and work to make something great happen, your chances increase drastically. When you think in terms of patience, think about when you are making things happen. There are times when being patient is better than taking the initiative. For instance, when you present an offer and they say they will call you next week, do not call them the next day. Wait until next week when it is appropriate to take the initiative again. You must build the skill of knowing when to wait and when to take action. Taking action beats patience nine times out of ten. Good things will come to those who wait, but only after taking action to earn that opportunity to practice patience.

How did I receive something great from patience?
What were my actions which lead up to that?

_____

_____

_____

_____

_____

How did I receive something great from taking action?
What did I do?

_____

_____

_____

_____

_____

What do I need to be more patient with?
What do I need to take action on?

_____

_____

_____

_____

_____

You miss 100% of the shots you don't take.

~ Wayne Gretzky ~

The answer to every question you do not ask will always be no. How can you score a goal in hockey if you never shoot? You have to take chances. You have to take risks. You have to get comfortable going out of your comfort zone. Taking those shots you have never taken before will be uncomfortable at first, but like anything, in time, it will become second nature to take the shots you know you should take. Get comfortable with asking the so-called stupid questions; you never know what opportunities may present themselves. Think in terms of action, now. Every time you do not go out and take a shot at an idea you have, it will never happen. You will never get a job unless you take a shot and apply. You will never date unless you take a shot and ask them out. Take that shot. Now!

What stopped me from taking that "shot" I am still thinking about?

_____

_____

_____

_____

_____

What "shot" have I not taken which I will take this week?

_____

_____

_____

_____

_____

What is the worst that could happen if I miss after taking the "shot"?

_____

_____

_____

_____

_____

Don't be afraid to give up the good to go for the great.

~ John D. Rockefeller ~

When you go for the greatness life has to offer, you will be risking everything that you know right now. You will either fail and lose everything, or you could become one of the most successful people the world has seen. It is good to be in a safe career with benefits, but it is great to create your own job, hire employees, and be an important part in supporting many families. It is good to live your life the way society dictates; it is great to go against the norm and become successful. Being good is simply average. Anyone can experience something good. Only those who risk and sacrifice are the ones who become great. Greatness is something the majority of people fail to even attempt once, though we all want it. The great become great because they go out and do great things with their great ideas for decades until they become a global reality.

What greatness am I living right now?

_____

_____

_____

_____

_____

What greatness do I want to achieve?

_____

_____

_____

_____

_____

What good things will I give up to become great?
(TV, video games, cell phone, fiction books, etc. included!)

_____

_____

_____

_____

_____

Even if you're on the right track, you'll get run over if you just sit there.

~ Will Rogers ~

Every day we are presented with millions of different choices. You may already be making all the right decisions which put you on the right track. If you do not take action every day, or at a minimum every week, you will get passed up by other people who are diligently working hard when you are out with your friends. No matter what you are working on, someone somewhere is doing what you are trying to do. If you sit idly by, they will run you over and be the successful one. Every day, do one thing that will take you closer to your desired outcome; do ten things if you can. There are numerous distractions that will get you run over by others: TV, news, video games, social media, drinking, drugs, laziness, procrastination, celebrity pop news, holidays, weekends, politics, and more. Start eliminating the junk from your life, and make time for success!

What junk do I waste my potential on?

_____

_____

_____

_____

_____

What time wasters can I eliminate out of my life?

_____

_____

_____

_____

_____

What can I work on instead of just "sitting on the tracks"?

_____

_____

_____

_____

_____

If you can breathe, you can achieve!

~ Lucas J. Robak ~

If you breathe, you are alive. If you are alive, there is nothing stopping you from achieving—except for you. There will be obstacles along the way that will prevent you from easily accomplishing what you are pursuing, but that is what is great about life. When you hit obstacles, your thinking gets stretched, and your horizons expand in order to achieve the outcome you desire. To achieve all of your wildest dreams, it is as simple as believing in yourself. Once you believe you can do it, the next step is to do it. Start, and see it through to the end. In achieving the outcome, your greatest accomplishment will be what you learned along the way. Yes, your outcome will become reality, but the most important part is who you become on the path to success. You will be stronger, smarter, and more creative than before.

What have I achieved in the past which I am proud of?

_____

_____

_____

_____

_____

What do I need to do differently to achieve what I am currently working on?

_____

_____

_____

_____

_____

What would I like to achieve in the future which I haven't started yet?
What are my first three steps?

_____

_____

_____

_____

_____

" In any situation, the best thing you can do is the right thing; the next best thing you can do is the wrong thing; the worst thing you can do is nothing.

~ Theodore Roosevelt ~

By doing nothing, you will get nothing. By doing the wrong thing, you at least did something, and were able to learn from it. Obviously, doing the right thing is best in any situation. To know what is right in every situation is easier than you think; follow your instincts and conscience. If you feel like something is wrong, do not do it. When some problem arises, you have three options: do the right thing, do the wrong thing, or do nothing. When you do nothing, you are allowing life to control what happens to you. In doing so, you have no say in what happens to your life and you now have zero right to complain about anything. When you do what is right, or even wrong, you are at least taking back control of your life. No matter what happens and what you do, learn from what led up to that situation, and what happened when you took action. Learn from the feedback life hands you and grow as a person.

What happened after I did not take action?
Am I happy with those results?

_____

_____

_____

_____

In a situation where I did what was right,
how did I know that was the right thing to do?

_____

_____

_____

_____

When I did the wrong thing in a situation that called for action,
what did I learn from the results?
How will I do it differently when I create that chance again?

_____

_____

_____

_____

It does not matter how slowly you go as long as you do not stop.

~ *Confucius* ~

If you start in Milwaukee, Wisconsin, and every day you take one step south, then sit down until the next day when you do it again, you cannot deny that one day you will end up in Chicago, Illinois. You could also choose to take five or ten steps a day; or three a week. You will eventually make it to your destination, as long as you do not stop. The same applies to anything you are trying to accomplish in life. Take three steps toward your goal once a day, or ten steps a day, whatever your schedule and your desire calls for. There may be times when you feel like you are going backwards which can be very frustrating. Do not stop! Do not give up! Do not quit! Keep moving forward no matter how hard it may be. As long as you send that one e-mail or make that one phone call that you need to each day, it will take you one step closer to accomplishing your goal.

How many steps a week can I realistically do?

_____

_____

_____

_____

_____

How many steps a day can I realistically do?

_____

_____

_____

_____

_____

What is one thing (or ten) I can do before I go to bed tonight?

_____

_____

_____

_____

_____

Either you run the day, or the day runs you.

~ Jim Rohn ~

It all boils down to using your time productively. You have twenty-four hours in a day. With eight hours of sleep, you have sixteen hours a day, giving you 112 hours in a week to be productive with a healthy sleep cycle. Since you only have sixteen hours a day, stop using it aimlessly; live it with purpose. Time is one thing we can never get back or make more of. No matter how wealthy you are, you do not know when your time bank will abruptly run out. You have the control to run your day by accomplishing the tasks that you want to. The day runs you through traffic, e-mail, phone calls, texts, weather, and anything else that happens in life. Your taking control to run the day can entail listening to audio books while driving; scheduling a time of day for e-mails, phone calls, texting, and social media; and checking the weather the night before. Control your life, or life will control you!

How can I, or how do I, control "traffic"?

_____

_____

_____

_____

_____

How can I, or how do I, control technology?

_____

_____

_____

_____

_____

What is uncontrollable in my life?
How can I control it?
(The answer,"I Can't" is not an answer)

_____

_____

_____

_____

_____

If you do what you've always done, you'll get what you've always gotten.

~ Tony Robbins ~

This sounds obvious, right? Right! Yet we keep doing the same things and expecting different results. Albert Einstein called that insanity. This applies to relationships, careers, goals, diets…everything! If you ask someone to do something and they do not do it, raising your voice and saying the same thing will not bring different results, you need to reframe the question or statement. If you keep having terrible relationships, you may have to start your next relationship differently; try refraining from sex for a few years to build a solid base—the divorce rate proves the American society is "insanely stupid" in this area. If you are always broke, maybe you need to invest your money instead of buying a pair of shoes you will not wear next year. The top three things people worry about most are their finances, health, and relationships. To improve them, start doing things differently. It's that simple!

How can I start treating my relationships differently?

_____

_____

_____

_____

How can I start treating my health differently?

_____

_____

_____

_____

How can I start treating my finances differently?
(Those still in school, develop good habits now!)

_____

_____

_____

_____

Opportunities don't happen, you create them.

~ Chris Grosser ~

People whom you consider lucky are not lucky; they worked hard, and took advantage of every opportunity presented to them to produce their own luck. You too can create your own luck by creating your own opportunities. Keep your goals in the front of your mind all day, every day; you will see opportunities you have never seen before. There may be someone you have seen hundreds of times over the years, even someone you do not know, yet that person could be one of your greatest opportunities. To make that person into an opportunity, you must talk to them, and know what you want! Creating opportunities is easy; all it takes is courage to do what others will not. It means doing affirmations every morning and every night before bed. An affirmation is a short, positive, present tense statement of your goal. Doing this will keep your dreams in your mind all day, reminding you to create new opportunities that were always there, but you had not noticed.

What opportunities have I created in the past?

_____

_____

_____

_____

_____

What opportunities have I passed up because I did not have the courage?

_____

_____

_____

_____

_____

Besides affirmations, how am I going to create my next opportunity?

_____

_____

_____

_____

_____

If opportunity doesn't knock, build a door.

~ Milton Berle ~

Every time you wake up, you wake up to opportunity. What is that opportunity? It is you; your thoughts, your passions, your dreams. You create all the circumstances in your life, which means you were the one who created all the opportunities that came your way. Make it your business to know the right people, make it your job to obtain the right skills, network in the right groups, do your research, get out of your comfort zone. Getting out of your comfort zone is the only way to create opportunities for yourself. If other people do not give you the opportunity, create your own opportunities by meeting the right people who will give you the time to manifest your desires. Other people have their own hopes and dreams they are pursuing. To make yours a reality, you will have to create your own opportunities with hard work, action, and persistence.

What three opportunities do I need to make me happier?

_____

_____

_____

_____

_____

Who can give me those opportunities?
What is their company, position, name, and/or job title?

_____

_____

_____

_____

How can I make those opportunities happen?
What steps do I need to take?

_____

_____

_____

_____

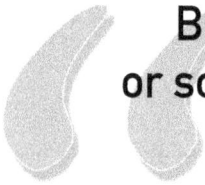

Build your own dreams, or someone else will hire you to build theirs.

~ Farrah Gray ~

The difference between the super successful and the average person is that the super successful make their dreams reality, and the average person works for them. This does not mean every employee or small business owner is average; they could very well be living their dream. The top 1 percent of people considered to be the richest in the world are told by the media that they need to pay their fair share. Is it really fair for someone to work as hard as they did to achieve their dreams, employ thousands, only to pay the average person not to work or try as hard as they did? When you build your own dreams, it is likely that you will hire people to help you build that dream. Stop helping other people build their dreams, start building yours. Do not worry; there are enough average people to go around to help every go-getter!

What dream am I building that is not mine?

_____

_____

_____

_____

_____

What dream of mine can I start building?
What are my first three steps?

_____

_____

_____

_____

_____

What can I delegate to others to help build my dream?

_____

_____

_____

_____

_____

"Your time is limited, so don't waste it living someone else's life.

~ Steve Jobs ~

The rest of the statement after the quote is, "Don't be trapped by dogma—which is living with the results of other people's thinking. Don't let the noise of others' opinions drown out your own inner voice. And most important, have the courage to follow your heart and intuition. They somehow already know what you truly want to become. Everything else is secondary."

This quote is from Steve Jobs' commencement address at Stanford in 2005. Look within yourself to find the answers to your life questions. Take twenty minutes each day to meditate for the answers, and you will find them. Your time is precious, treat it as such.

What results am I living that are from other people's thinking?

_____

_____

_____

_____

_____

How does my heart want me to live?

_____

_____

_____

_____

_____

What is my intuition telling me?

_____

_____

_____

_____

_____

"What you do speaks so loudly that I cannot hear what you say.

~ Ralph Waldo Emerson ~

Actions speak louder than words. Both your words and your actions affect everyone around you. If you tell someone you will do something, be good to your word and do it. If in the past you have not been good to your word, acknowledge that fact and forgive yourself. Don't beat yourself up or go into seclusion about it. Focus on today, and the actions you do daily. Take the third-person view. What actions do you take that others see? Keep your word and your actions congruent. It is better to say nothing or say "no," than promise to do something and then not do it. Your word and your actions affect everyone around you. It does not matter if you spend all day in bed or go out and volunteer. When you seclude yourself, you affect those you could have met by your absence. In the end, you change the world by your actions, or inaction.

How can I say "no" when I know I won't follow through?

_____

_____

_____

_____

_____

How did people react after my actions did not back up my words?
(Vice Versa too!)

_____

_____

_____

_____

How did I view other people who acted
in a way contrary to what was said?

_____

_____

_____

_____

Luck is a dividend of sweat.
The more you sweat, the luckier you get.

~ Ray Kroc ~

There is no such thing as a lucky person. Luck is purely a state of mind. When two people get into a car accident, the lucky person is grateful to be alive, the unlucky person sees only a totaled car and hospital bills. In a raffle, a lucky person does not care if they lose and is happy for the winner; an unlucky person gets upset, and says the drawing was rigged. You call some people lucky because everything is going well for them. But that luck did not appear out of thin air; they worked hard when everyone else was out living life. While you were wasting your life in front of a TV set, they were working up a sweat creating their luck. Remember: when you are doing nothing, there is always someone out there working harder than you to accomplish what you are putting off.

What luck have I created from hard work?

_____

_____

_____

_____

_____

What luck did I receive from doing absolutely nothing?

_____

_____

_____

_____

_____

What can I do to create my own luck?

_____

_____

_____

_____

_____

The difference between ordinary and extraordinary is that little extra.

~ Jimmy Johnson ~

Take the initiative. Go above and beyond of what is expected of you. Put in a little more effort than everyone else. At work, be the first to arrive and the last to leave. There are many ways of reframing this, but they all mean the same thing. Ordinary is average, and average people don't stand out in your mind. When you receive service that is above and beyond anything you experienced, you will remember it, and look at the person providing that service as extraordinary. You can do this in all areas of life; from school to work, from friends to family, from walking down the street to being a customer. No one wants to be average and ordinary, yet very few people actually make that extra effort to stand out from the rest. In the 21st Century, becoming that extraordinary person is getting easier and easier! Give everything "that little extra."

What have I noticed when people put in that little extra?

_____

_____

_____

_____

_____

Where and how can I start putting in extra effort?

_____

_____

_____

_____

_____

What benefits will I directly receive from going above and beyond?

_____

_____

_____

_____

_____

Successful people do what unsuccessful people are not willing to do. Don't wish it were easier, wish you were better.

~ Jim Rohn ~

Becoming a success requires an investment of time and effort. Successful people driven with passion invest as much as 60 to 110 hours per week in their vision and their plan. The average person without a vision works dispassionately, 40 hours or less per week, putting their efforts into someone else's plan. There is a saying, "I'd rather work 80 hours a week so that I don't have to work 40." For successful people, hard work is a choice and has purpose, and that purpose brings joy. For average people, work is an obligation and hard, something to endure, a drudgery to suffer. Successful people are consumed with what they are passionate about, and work hard on their plan to achieve their goals. Average people have no plan and no goals, give away their passion without aim, and when faced with obstacles, give up. Successful people channel their passion into facing obstacles head on, and overcoming them. Average people do nothing with their ideas. Successful people buy time, average people sell their time. Successful people pursue their ideas and turn them into reality. Who do you want to be?

What am I willing to do that successful people do?

_____

_____

_____

_____

_____

What do I already do that unsuccessful people are not willing to do?

_____

_____

_____

_____

_____

What can I do to be better than the average person?

_____

_____

_____

_____

_____

The question isn't who is going to let me; it's who is going to stop me.

~ Ayn Rand ~

If someone does not allow you to do something, do it anyway! People have a tendency to become roadblocks for other people's goals. When you encounter such human roadblocks, you have several options. You can go above them, meaning go to the people who are superiors of the person who just shot you down. You can go around them, meaning do it anyway, but stay off their radar so they do not block you again. You can go under them, meaning proceed with what you wanted to do with the support and knowledge of those who are below the roadblock in power. You can go right through them, meaning you proceed with what you want to do right in front of them, making sure they know you are doing what they told you not to do. There are many examples in real life of how others went above, around, under, or right through people who were roadblocks. Choose the path that applies to you! Never let anyone stop you from achieving; they are too small minded to know better.

Who are the people in my life who will try and stop me?

_____

_____

_____

_____

_____

What will I do next time someone tries to stop me?
(Be specific, not metaphorical)

_____

_____

_____

_____

How can I get past my current roadblocks?

_____

_____

_____

_____

Success is the sum of small efforts, repeated day in and day out.

~ Robert Collier ~

A mason is someone who lays bricks to build walls, buildings, walkways, etc. If a mason laid one brick every day during his whole career, by the end of his career, he would have built a great wall or building. The small effort of laying one brick every day eventually adds up to a great achievement. You can do this, too. Figure out what you want to do, and take one step a day to make it happen. Or you can do one step a week, or even three. Depending upon your desire to change your life, you can go as far as taking twenty steps a day. All the small efforts you put forth will eventually add up to one great success. Add up your pennies, and they will eventually make a dollar.

How many steps can I realistically do every week?
Every day?

_____

_____

_____

_____

_____

What time do I have available during the week to take these steps?
What time do I have during the weekend?

_____

_____

_____

_____

_____

What can I sacrifice to free up time to accomplish more?

_____

_____

_____

_____

_____

The most difficult thing is the decision to act, the rest is merely tenacity.

~ Amelia Earhart ~

Tenacity: Not easily stopped or pulled apart…firm or strong…continuing for a long time…very determined to do something. ~ Merriam-Webster

Think back to when you were in school and had homework to do. The hardest part about homework was starting. The decision to start is the hardest thing to do in all areas of life. Once you start, you will build momentum within yourself to keep going. To build that momentum, you have to be strong and continue for a long time. Your determination to see it to the end will get stronger, and you will not be easily pulled off your task. Tenacity is only important after you first act!

What experience have I encountered where
I was tenacious and succeeded?

_____

_____

_____

_____

_____

What is the hardest thing for me to start right now?

_____

_____

_____

_____

_____

How will I and my environment benefit from the completion
of what I am "waiting" to start?

_____

_____

_____

_____

_____

Happiness is not something ready-made. It comes from your own actions.

~ Dalai Lama ~

Happiness in life is not guaranteed; you have to make the appropriate choices that are relevant to you and your dreams in order to be happy. Your happiness in life comes from your thoughts and actions, not one or the other. Since happiness is a state of mind, a choice, it is all in your head. Your actions come from your thoughts which prompted your action. You cannot sit around waiting for happiness to come to you; go out and make things happen which will make you happy. Happiness is not a destination you should hope for; happiness is a part of the journey you take to get to the destination where you want to be. Happiness comes from doing, so do something that makes you happy and you will be happy.

What am I currently doing to make myself happy?

_____

_____

_____

_____

What thoughts make me happy?

_____

_____

_____

_____

What actions can I do to make myself happy
and spread happiness to others?

_____

_____

_____

_____

Never leave that till tomorrow which you can do today.

~ Benjamin Franklin ~

Yesterday is always in the past, tomorrow will never come; the only time you have is today, right now. Now is where the power is. When you have time to do something now, do not talk yourself into doing it tomorrow because chances are you will not do it. You will push it off for tomorrow time and time again. There is no time like the present because that is the only time you live in. The present, today, the immediate now, is all you have. You will have to go through with it at some point if you want to succeed. Going through the actions necessary to succeed only exist today, in the now, your immediate present. They do not exist in your tomorrows and yesterdays; yesterdays no longer matter. The NOW is the only thing that counts!

What have I been putting off for the "tomorrows" which never came?

_____

_____

_____

_____

_____

What have I accomplished in the present that I never did "tomorrow"?

_____

_____

_____

_____

_____

How can I get myself to start doing things today?

_____

_____

_____

_____

_____

Only put off until tomorrow what you are willing to die having left undone.

~ Pablo Picasso ~

As sad as it is, your life could end before you go to bed tonight. You might not wake up tomorrow. Tomorrow is full of uncertainty; you never know what day will be your last. The only time you have is now, today. Do what is important to you and leave the meaningless tasks for tomorrow. Plan out your days with tasks that mean something to you, something that will help change the lives of others. There is only so much time in a day and you spend eight hours of it sleeping. Every day you have sixteen hours to get the most important tasks of your life done. Every day, every second, is more important than the last because it could all be taken away at any second. Do what you need to do today; do not push it off for tomorrow. You may never get the chance.

What do I keep putting off that is more important
than watching tv, video games, social media, etc.?

_____

_____

_____

_____

_____

What do I need to do today?

_____

_____

_____

_____

If I die tomorrow, what will I regret never having done?

_____

_____

_____

_____

_____

ACTION NOTES

ACTION NOTES

CHAPTER TEN
PERSISTENCE

Persistence: The quality that allows someone to continue doing something, or trying to do something, even though it is difficult or opposed by other people...the state of occurring or existing beyond the usual, expected, or normal time. ~ Merriam-Webster

In psychological terms: Perseverance in spite of fatigue or frustration.
~ C.R. Cloninger ~

Persistence is measured in eagerness of effort, hard work, ambition, and perfectionism. Persistence "can also be measured as the time invested in staying on task," per *Wikipedia*. "If a cab driver works an 8-hour shift, their persistence is eight hours."

Someone who is persistent will keep going until the job is completed to his or her liking. Completion may require little to no effort, or it might need all your effort. Persistence does not mean effort; persistence means to keep going until it is done.

When you have endurance and stamina, with a desire to produce the life you want, it will only be a matter of time before you turn an idea into reality. After Bill Gates came up with the Microsoft technology in his teens, from 20 to 30 years of age he dedicated every day with tenacity and determination to create a multi-billion dollar empire. Even if you have a billion dollar idea like Bill Gates, Steve Jobs, Warren Buffet, Mark Cuban, Mark Zuckerberg, Richard Branson, etc., you need to persevere for a long time to turn it into something worth talking about.

Most of the important things in the world have been accomplished by people who have kept on trying when there seemed to be no hope at all.

~ Dale Carnegie ~

The secret to life is to keep going, keep trying. If your car breaks down on a road trip in the middle of nowhere, some may think there is no hope, and give up because they have not seen a car in hours. Do not give up on your life. Do not give up on your dreams. Do not give up on what is important to you. The great thing about life is that we are all different, which means we all have different ideas of what is important to us. The only way to fail is to give up and quit. Do not quit on what is important to you, that's a wicked habit to create. If it is important enough for you to try once, then it is important enough for you to finish so the rest of the world can benefit.

What is important to me that I gave up on?

_____

_____

_____

_____

_____

How bad do I want what I gave up on?

_____

_____

_____

_____

What is important for me to accomplish now?
Why?

_____

_____

_____

_____

_____

"Whenever you see a successful person, you only see the public glories, never the private sacrifices to reach them.

~ Vaibhav Shah ~

Sacrifice is a daily occurrence you may have never noticed before. When you go to school or work, you sacrifice hours you could be outside in the sun with your family and friends. When you play video games, you sacrifice reading a book, doing homework, or improving your life. When you go out with friends on the weekend, you sacrifice time to study or further your career. The public only sees the success a person creates. Successful people make sacrifices that average people think are impossible and inhumane. Entrepreneurs may sacrifice comfort by living in their office or car; valedictorians may sacrifice their weekends to study and do homework; career-oriented people may sacrifice family and friends to make it to the top; police officers and soldiers may sacrifice their lives to protect the greater good. Be conscientious of your decisions and what you are sacrificing.

What result producing activities do I need to do?

_____

_____

_____

_____

What are my biggest time wasters
which take me away from successful actions?
What should I sacrifice?

_____

_____

_____

_____

How I can enforce my boundaries with sacrificing
to focus on successful actions?

_____

_____

_____

_____

A successful man is one who can lay a firm foundation with the bricks that others throw at him.

~ Sidney Greenberg ~

Life will give you all sorts of obstacles that might prevent you from accomplishing your goal. Those who are successful take what life throws at them and build upon it. All your life experiences developed you into who you are today. With every situation and circumstance, you have millions of options to choose from. Choose to take what life throws at you and build a firm foundation of integrity, values, loyalty, honesty, responsibility, morality, ethics, and more. It is up to you to decide what to do, and how to respond to all the negativity you will encounter along your way to the top. Turn the negativity life hands you into something wonderful. You choose your own destiny every second. To manifest that destiny you desire, you must do the right thing every chance you get. Use the negativity to help you grow!

What bricks make up my foundation?

_____

_____

_____

_____

_____

What negative situation can I look at as a positive
for building a firmer foundation?

_____

_____

_____

_____

_____

What obstacle am I facing right now
which will help me grow into a better person?

_____

_____

_____

_____

_____

Success is a function of persistence and doggedness and the willingness to work hard for twenty-two minutes to make sense of something that most people would give up on after thirty seconds.

~ Malcolm Gladwell ~

Doggedness: a steadfast adherence to an opinion, purpose, or course of action in spite of reason, arguments, or persuasion.
~ Merriam-Webster

Success is your connection to goodwill, endurance, and self-will in order to labor intensely far longer than most people. Hypothetically speaking, if it only took twenty-two minutes to achieve the dreams you desire, the majority of people will give up within thirty seconds. By possessing a steadfast determination towards your end result, you will have the willingness to maintain directed focus creating an outcome of results. The average person can be given a step-by-step guide on how to achieve their desires and they would not even take "thirty seconds" worth of action on it. To become a success with whatever it is you are pursuing, make peace with the fact that it may take years longer than you expect. Hard work pays off in time, willingly put your "twenty-two minutes" of effort into your purpose while maintaining your course of action.

What challenges have I overcome with persistence?
What did I learn from those experiences?

_____

_____

_____

_____

_____

What challenges do I expect to encounter in the near future?
How will I overcome them?

_____

_____

_____

_____

_____

What is one thing I will put steadfast persistence towards
which the average person would give up on after barely trying?

_____

_____

_____

_____

_____

"I have not failed. I've just found ten thousand ways that won't work.

~ Thomas A. Edison ~

New and great ideas are a common occurrence. You have many great ideas each day. The possibility that the majority of people will make even one attempt to realize one of their millions of ideas is zero percent. Most people put zero effort into attempts at fulfilling their dreams. Most people do not try even once! To try and fail ten thousand times alone is success. Even if Thomas Edison had not invented the light bulb, he was a success for not just trying once, but persisting ten thousand times, learning from it, and trying again. You will never succeed until you try. How badly do you want it? How strong is your desire? Pursue what you are passionate about; then you will try a hundred thousand times until you succeed. When you fail, smile and know you succeeded in identifying one way that didn't work. Get up and do it again differently.

What motivated me to keep trying until I succeeded?

_____

_____

_____

_____

_____

What do I want to try again that I had given up on?

_____

_____

_____

_____

_____

What have I not tried yet which I keep thinking about?

_____

_____

_____

_____

_____

" I didn't fail the test.
I just found a hundred ways to do it wrong.

~ Benjamin Franklin ~

In the real world, every day, life is your test. If you fail the first time, you can keep trying until you get it right. There is no set number as to how many times you can try and fail at something until you succeed. When you try to do something and fail, pay attention to the feedback you get so you can do it differently next time, and the next, and the next. As long as you keep trying and applying the knowledge you get from the feedback, you will succeed; you will pass the test of life. Once you leave school, a whole new set of rules applies. You pass in the real world by trying over and over again, learning all the ways that do not work so you can find the one thing that does.

What have I accomplished after failing the first couple times?

_____

_____

_____

_____

_____

What did I fail and give up at which I should try again?

_____

_____

_____

_____

_____

How will I and my environment benefit from it?

_____

_____

_____

_____

_____

It's not whether you get knocked down, it's whether you get up.

~ *Vince Lombardi* ~

You will get knocked down, guaranteed. The only time you will not is when you do not try, or do not go after something worth going after. Getting knocked down in life is when you fail at your first attempt, or even your thousandth attempt. What defines you as a winner or a loser is what you do after you do not succeed. Instead of blaming others, complaining about everything that went wrong, or making excuses for your lack of preparation, get back out there and do it again with a new perspective on how to accomplish it. Getting knocked down, failing, is a gift. Failure is the best learning process life can give you. Get back up and go do it again!

What should I try again?

_____

_____

_____

_____

_____

What did I learn from my first attempt?
How am I going to do it differently?

_____

_____

_____

_____

How will I benefit from trying again?

_____

_____

_____

_____

_____

Fall seven times and stand up eight.

~ Japanese Proverb ~

Success is always one more try away. If you keep getting knocked down, get back up every time. If you fall seven times and get up seven times, you will get knocked down again. If you get up once more, there is a chance that the eighth time is when your success will come. Life will knock you down, and you will fall on your own; these are givens. You need to get back up and try again. The view at the top is far better than the view from the bottom. Think of the skyscrapers in New York City. From the ground, you are surrounded and feel small. When you get up to the hundredth floor or so, the view is spectacular, and feels like you are on top of the world. Keep getting back up, and the view will get better with each try!

What did I give up on after numerous attempts?

_____

_____

_____

_____

_____

What did I accomplish after numerous attempts?

_____

_____

_____

_____

_____

What "view" do I want for my life?

_____

_____

_____

_____

_____

If you're going through hell, keep going.

~ Winston Churchill ~

If you end up in a horrible situation, do you just sit there? No! Smart people, winners, will do what they can to get out of that situation; they keep moving forward. Everyone in life has been through hell, but few end up becoming a success. The ones who achieve success do so because they kept moving and doing what they believed to be right. Whenever we are put in a situation we do not want to be in, something we hate, it is in our nature to do what we can to get out of it and come out on whatever side we can. Then there are some people who will accept that they cannot get any better, or believe they do not deserve anything better. They end up living a life of hell every day, because they did not keep going. When you drive in a tunnel, eventually you will come out the other side if you keep moving in the right direction.

What "hell" have I accepted in life?

_____

_____

_____

_____

_____

How is accepting this "hell" better than moving forward?

_____

_____

_____

_____

_____

What do I need to do to get out of that "hell"?

_____

_____

_____

_____

_____

PERSISTENCE NOTES

PERSISTENCE NOTES

REFERENCED BIOGRAPHIES

All bios were copy and pasted from the first paragraph on Wikipedia in April 2014 unless otherwise indicated after the short description in parenthesis.

The names are arranged alphabetically by last name. You will see the first name is included before their last name.

After copy and pasting from Wikipedia and other sources, the content has been cleaned up by taking out words and symbols that were irrelevant to you getting the general idea of who they are.

Feel free to research any person you want in greater detail. This is meant to give you an extremely brief overview of who the person is.

-A-

Anonymous (pg.4, 74, 78, 172) - Anonymous works are works, such as art or literature, that have an anonymous, undisclosed, or unknown creator or author. In the United States it is legally defined as "a work on the copies or phono-records of which no natural person is identified as author." In the case of very old works, the author's name may simply be lost over the course of history and time. In such cases the author is often referred to as Anonymous, the Latin form of "anonymous". In the case of works where the creator's name is kept secret, the author's reasons may vary from fear of persecution to protection of his or her reputation.

Aristotle (pg.28, 58) – (384 – 322 BCE) was a Greek philosopher born in Stagirus, northern Greece, in 384 BCE. His father, Nicomachus, died when Aristotle was a child, whereafter Proxenus of Atarneus became his guardian. At eighteen, he joined Plato's Academy in Athens and remained there until the age of thirty-seven (347 BCE). His writings cover many subjects – including physics, biology, zoology, metaphysics, logic, ethics, aesthetics, poetry, theater, music, rhetoric, linguistics, politics and government.

-B-

Richard Bach (pg.6) - (born June 23, 1937) is an American writer. He is widely known as the author of the hugely popular 1970s best-sellers Jonathan Livingston Seagull and Illusions: The Adventures of a Reluctant Messiah, among others. Bach's books espouse his philosophy that our apparent physical limits and mortality are merely appearance. Bach is noted for his love of flying and for his books related to air flight and flying in a metaphorical context. He has pursued flying as a hobby since the age of 17. In late August 2012 Bach was badly injured when on approach to landing at Friday Harbor his aircraft clipped some power lines and crashed upside down in a field.

Richard Wayne Bandler (pg.48) - (born February 24, 1950) is an American author and trainer in the field of self-help. He is best known as the co-creator (with John Grinder) of Neuro-linguistic programming (NLP), a methodology to understand and change human behavior-patterns. He also developed other systems named Design Human Engineering (DHE) and Neuro Hypnotic Repatterning (NHR).

Milton Berle (pg.192) – (born Milton Berlinger; July 12, 1908 – March 27, 2002) was an American comedian and actor. As the host of NBC's Texaco Star Theater (1948–55), he was the first major American television star and was known to millions of viewers as "Uncle Miltie" and "Mr. Television" during TV's golden age.

Michael John Bobak (pg.104) - Mainly worked as an engineer from the late 60s (From http://www.discogs.com/). If you find more information of Michael John Bobak, please contact: Lucas@LucasRobak.com

Leslie C. "Les" Brown (pg.94) - (born February 17, 1945) is a motivational speaker, former Ohio politician, popular author, radio DJ, and former host of The Les Brown Show. As a politician, he is a former member of the Ohio House of Representatives. As a motivational speaker, he uses the catch phrase, "It's possible," and teaches people to follow their dreams as he learned to do.

Gautama Buddha (pg.86) - also known as Siddhārtha Gautama, Shakyamuni, or simply the Buddha, was a sage on whose teachings Buddhism was founded. Born in the Shakya republic in the Himalayan foothills, Gautama. Buddha taught primarily in north-eastern India. Buddha means "awakened one" or "the enlightened one.""Buddha" is also used as a title for the first awakened being in an era. In most Buddhist traditions, Siddhartha Gautama is regarded as the Supreme. Gautama taught a Middle Way between sensual indulgence and the severe asceticism found in the Sramana (renunciation) movement common in his region. He later taught throughout regions of eastern India such as Magadha and Kośala. Gautama is the primary figure in Buddhism, and accounts of his life, discourses, and monastic rules are believed by Buddhists to have been summarized after his death and memorized by his followers. Various collections of teachings attributed to him were passed down by oral tradition, and first committed to writing about 400 years later.

Henry Thomas Buckle (pg.128) - (24 November 1821 – 29 May 1862) was an English historian, author of an unfinished History of Civilization and a very strong amateur chess player.

-C-

Dale Breckenridge Carnegie (pg.116, 222) – (spelled Carnagey until c. 1922) (November 24, 1888 – November 1, 1955) was an American writer and lecturer and the developer of famous courses in self-improvement, salesmanship, corporate training, public speaking, and interpersonal skills. Born into poverty on a farm in Missouri, he was the author of How to Win Friends and Influence People (1936), a massive bestseller that remains popular today. He also wrote How to Stop Worrying and Start Living (1948), Lincoln the Unknown (1932), and several other books. One of the core ideas in his books is that it is possible to change other people's behavior by changing one's behavior toward them.

Sir Winston Leonard Spencer-Churchill (pg.50, 238) - (30 November 1874 – 24 January 1965) was a British politician who was the Prime Minister of the United Kingdom from 1940 to 1945 and again from 1951 to 1955. Widely regarded as one of the greatest wartime leaders of the 20th century, Churchill was also an officer in the British Army, a historian, a writer, and an artist. He is the only British Prime Minister to have won the Nobel Prize in Literature, and was the first person to be made an honorary citizen of the United States.

Robert Collier (pg.208) - (April 19, 1885 in St. Louis, Missouri - 1950) was an American author of self-help, and New Thought metaphysical books in the 20th century. He was the nephew of Peter Fenelon Collier, founder of Collier's Weekly. He was involved in writing, editing, and research for most of his life. His book The Secret of the Ages (1926) sold over 300,000 copies during his life. Collier wrote about the practical psychology of abundance, desire, faith, visualization, confident action, and becoming your best.

Confucius (pg.184) - (551–479 BC) was a Chinese teacher, editor, politician, and philosopher of the Spring and Autumn period of Chinese history. The philosophy of Confucius emphasized personal and governmental morality, correctness of social relationships, justice and sincerity. His followers competed successfully with many other schools during the Hundred Schools of Thought Era only to be suppressed in favor of the Legalists during the Qin Dynasty. Following the victory of Hanover Chu after the collapse of Qin, Confucius's thoughts received official sanction and were further developed into a system known as Confucianism.

William John (Bill) Copeland (pg.156) - (16 August 1929 – 20 September 2011) was an Australian Test cricket match umpire, from Warrnambool, Victoria. He umpired 1 Test match in 1980 between Australia and England at Sydney on 4 January to 8 January 1980, a low-scoring game with bowlers Dennis Lillee, Geoff Dymock, and Len Pascoe giving Australia a victory by 6 wickets, after a number of controversial decisions went against England. Copeland's partner was Robin Bailhache. Copeland umpired one One Day International (ODI) match in December 1979. In January 1979 he umpired one women's Test match. Altogether, he umpired 14 first-class matches in his career between 1973 and 1980, the Test match being his last. Off the field Copeland was a member of the Victorian police force.

Stephen Richards Covey (pg.40) - (October 24, 1932 – July 16, 2012) was an American educator, author, businessman, and keynote speaker. His most popular book was The Seven Habits of Highly Effective People. His other books include First Things First, Principle-Centered Leadership, The Seven Habits of Highly Effective Families, The 8th Habit, and The Leader In Me — How Schools and Parents Around the World Are Inspiring Greatness, One Child at a Time. He was a professor at the Jon M. Huntsman School of Business at Utah State University at the time of his death.

-D-

Sir Colin Rex Davis (pg.112) - (25 September 1927 – 14 April 2013) was an English conductor best known for his association with the London Symphony Orchestra, having first conducted it in 1959. His repertoire was broad, but among the composers with whom he was particularly associated were Mozart, Berlioz, Elgar, Sibelius, Stravinsky and Tippett. He studied as a clarinettist, but was intent on becoming a conductor. After struggles as a freelance conductor from 1949 to 1957, he gained a series of appointments with orchestras including the BBC Scottish Orchestra, the BBC Symphony Orchestra and the Bavarian Radio Symphony Orchestra. He also held the musical directorships of Sadler's Wells Opera and the Royal Opera House, where he was principal conductor for over fifteen years. His guest conductorships included the Boston Symphony Orchestra, the New York Philharmonic and the Staatskapelle Dresden, among many others. As a teacher, Davis held posts at the Royal Academy of Music, London, and the Hochschule für Musik Carl Maria von Weber (conservatory) in Dresden. He made his first gramophone recordings in 1958, and his discography over the next five decades was extensive, with a large number of studio recordings for Philips Records and a substantial catalog of live recordings for the London Symphony Orchestra's own label.

Walter Elias "Walt" Disney (pg.162) - (December 5, 1901 – December 15, 1966) was an American business magnate, animator, cartoonist, producer, director, screenwriter, philanthropist and voice actor. A major figure within the American animation industry and throughout the world, he is regarded as an international icon, well known for his influence and contributions to the field of entertainment during the 20th century. As a Hollywood business mogul, he, along with his brother Roy O. Disney, co-founded Walt Disney Productions, which later became one of the best-known motion picture production companies in the world. The corporation is now known as The Walt Disney Company and had an annual revenue of approximately US$45 billion in the 2013 financial year.

-E-

Amelia Mary Earhart (pg.210) - (July 24, 1897 – disappeared July 2, 1937) was an American aviation pioneer and author. Earhart was the first female aviator to fly solo across the Atlantic Ocean. She received the U.S.

Distinguished Flying Cross for this record. She set many other records, wrote best-selling books about her flying experiences and was instrumental in the formation of The Ninety-Nines, an organization for female pilots. Earhart joined the faculty of the Purdue University aviation department in 1935 as a visiting faculty member to counsel women on careers and help inspire others with her love for aviation. She was also a member of the National Woman's Party, and an early supporter of the Equal Rights Amendment.

Thomas Alva Edison (pg.114, 230) - (February 11, 1847 – October 18, 1931) was an American inventor and businessman. He developed many devices that greatly influenced life around the world, including the phonograph, the motion picture camera, and a long-lasting, practical electric light bulb. Dubbed "The Wizard of Menlo Park", he was one of the first inventors to apply the principles of mass production and large-scale teamwork to the process of invention, and because of that, he is often credited with the creation of the first industrial research laboratory.

Albert Einstein (pg.20, 120, 130) - (14 March 1879 – 18 April 1955) was a German-born theoretical physicist. He developed the general theory of relativity, one of the two pillars of modern physics (alongside quantum mechanics). While best known for his mass–energy equivalence formula=mc2 (which has been dubbed "the world's most famous equation"), he received the 1921 Nobel Prize in Physics "for his services to theoretical physics, and especially for his discovery of the law of the photoelectric effect". The latter was pivotal in establishing quantum theory.

George Eliot (pg.170) - Mary Ann Evans (22 November 1819 – 22 December 1880; alternatively "Mary Anne" or "Marian"), known by her pen name George Eliot, was an English novelist, journalist, translator and one of the leading writers of the Victorian era. She is the author of seven novels, including Adam Bede (1859), The Mill on the Floss (1860), Silas Marner (1861), Middlemarch (1871-72), and Daniel Deronda (1876), most set in provincial England and known for their realism and psychological insight.

Ralph Waldo Emerson (pg.2, 8, 18, 198) - (May 25, 1803 – April 27, 1882) was an American essayist, lecturer, and poet, who led the Transcendentalist movement of the mid-19th century. He was seen as a champion of individualism and a prescient critic of the countervailing pressures of society, and he disseminated his thoughts through dozens of published essays and more than 1,500 public lectures across the United States.

-F-

Henry Ford (pg.24, 38) - (July 30, 1863 – April 7, 1947) was an American industrialist, the founder of the Ford Motor Company, and sponsor of the development of the assembly line technique of mass production. Although Ford did not invent the automobile or the assembly line, he developed and manufactured the first automobile that many middle class Americans could afford. In doing so, Ford converted the automobile from an expensive curiosity into a practical conveyance that would profoundly impact the landscape of the twentieth century. His introduction of the Model T automobile revolutionized transportation and American industry. As owner of the Ford Motor Company, he became one of the richest and best-known people in the world. He is credited with "Fordism": mass production of inexpensive goods coupled with high wages for workers. Ford had a global vision, with consumerism as the key to peace. His intense commitment to systematically lowering costs resulted in many technical and business innovations, including a franchise system that put dealerships throughout most of North America and in major cities on six continents. Ford left most of his vast wealth to the Ford Foundation and arranged for his family to control the company permanently.

Anatole France (pg.150) - (16 April 1844 – 12 October 1924) was a French poet, journalist, and novelist. He was born in Paris, and died in Saint-Cyr-sur-Loire. He was a successful novelist, with several best-sellers. Ironic and skeptical, he was considered in his day the ideal French man of letters. He was a member of the Académie française, and won the Nobel Prize for Literature in recognition of his literary achievements. France is also widely believed to be the model for narrator Marcel's literary idol Bergotte in Marcel Proust's In Search of Lost Time.

Benjamin Franklin (pg.214, 232) – (January 6, 1705– April 17, 1790) was one of the Founding Fathers of the United States and in many ways was "the First American". A world-famous polymath, Franklin was a leading author, printer, political theorist, politician, postmaster, scientist, inventor, civic activist, statesman, and diplomat. As a scientist, he was a major figure in the American Enlightenment and the history of physics for his discoveries and theories regarding electricity. As an inventor, he is known for the lightning rod, bifocals, and the Franklin stove, among other inventions. He facilitated many civic organizations, including Philadelphia's fire department and a university.

Robert Lee Frost (pg.12) - (March 26, 1874 – January 29, 1963) was an American poet. His work was initially published in England before it was published in America. He is highly regarded for his realistic depictions of rural life and his command of American colloquial speech. His work frequently employed settings from rural life in New England in the early twentieth century, using them to examine complex social and philosophical themes. One of the most popular and critically respected American poets of the twentieth century, Frost was honored frequently during his lifetime, receiving four Pulitzer Prizes for Poetry. He became one of America's rare "public literary figures, almost an artistic institution."

-G-

Malcolm Gladwell (pg.228) - (born September 3, 1963) - is a Canadian journalist, bestselling author, and speaker. He has been a staff writer for The New Yorker since 1996. He has written five books, The Tipping Point: How Little Things Can Make a Big Difference (2000), Blink: The Power of Thinking Without Thinking (2005), Outliers: The Story of Success (2008),What the Dog Saw: And Other Adventures (2009), a collection of his journalism, and David and Goliath: Underdogs, Misfits, and the Art of Battling Giants (2013). All five books were on The New York Times Best Seller list. Gladwell's books and articles often deal with the unexpected implications of research in the social sciences and make frequent and extended use of academic work, particularly in the areas of sociology, psychology, and social psychology. Gladwell was appointed to the Order of Canada on June 30, 2011.

Ray Goforth (pg.134) - the assertive leader of 23,000 unionized technical staff at Boeing, has created a "different dynamic" in contract talks with the company. (http://seattletimes.com/html/businesstechnology/)

Farrah Gray (pg.194) – (born Farrakhan Khalid Muhammad) is an American businessman, investor, philanthropist, author, columnist, and motivational speaker. He was named as one of the most influential black men in America by the National Urban League. Gray was raised on Chicago's South side. He began his entrepreneurial career at the age of six selling homemade lotion and hand-painted rocks door-to-door.

Sidney Greenberg (pg.226) - (September 27, 1917-March 31, 2003) was an American rabbi and author. A native New Yorker, he spent more than 50 years as Rabbi of Temple Sinai, now in Dresher, Pennsylvania. He received his undergraduate degree from Yeshiva University, and his rabbinical ordination, and later, a Doctor of Hebrew Literature degree, from Jewish Theological Seminary of America, in New York. He wrote numerous books on Judaism, and wrote several prayer books.

Wayne Douglas Gretzky (pg.174) - (born January 26, 1961) is a Canadian former professional ice hockey player and former head coach. He played 20 seasons in the National Hockey League (NHL) for four teams from 1979 to 1999. Nicknamed "The Great One", he has been called "the greatest hockey player ever" by many sportswriters, players, and the NHL itself. He is the leading point-scorer in NHL history, with more assists than any other player has points, and is the only NHL player to total over 200 points in one season – a feat he accomplished four times. In addition, he tallied over 100 points in 16 professional seasons, 14 of them consecutive. At the time of his retirement in 1999, he held 40 regular-season records, 15 playoff records, and six All-Star records.

Chris Grosser (pg.190) - Chris Grosser Photography was founded and launched in 2007. During the time of his company's launch, Chris was 18 years of age while simultaneously completing his under-graduate degree from the University of South Florida, studying Business & Marketing. The foundation of Chris Grosser Photography was built on a passion for photography and an insatiable desire to capture the world around him.

-H-

Napoleon Hill (pg.64, 106, 136, 140) - (October 26, 1883 – November 8, 1970) was an American author in the area of the new thought movement who was one of the earliest producers of the modern genre of personal-success literature. He is widely considered to be one of the great writers on success. His most famous work, Think and Grow Rich (1937), is one of the best-selling books of all time (at the time of Hill's death in 1970, Think and Grow Rich had sold 20 million copies). Hill's works examined the power of personal beliefs, and the role they play in personal success. He became an advisor to President Franklin D. Roosevelt from 1933 to 1936. "What the mind of man can conceive and believe, it can achieve" is one of Hill's hallmark expressions. How achievement actually occurs, and a formula for it that puts success in reach of the average person, were the focal points of Hill's books.

Elbert Hubbard (pg.138) - (June 19, 1856 – May 7, 1915) was an American writer, publisher, artist, and philosopher. Raised in Hudson, Illinois, he had early success as a traveling salesman for the Larkin Soap Company. Presently Hubbard is known best as the initiator of the Roycroft artisan community in East Aurora, New York, a realization of the Arts and Crafts philosophy. Among his many publications were the nine-volume work Little Journeys to the Homes of the Great and the short publication A Message to Garcia. He and his second wife, Alice Moore Hubbard, died aboard the RMS Lusitania, when it was sunk by a German submarine off the coast of Ireland on May 7, 1915.

-J-

Steven Paul "Steve" Jobs (pg.196) - (February 24, 1955 – October 5, 2011) was an American entrepreneur, marketer, and inventor, who was the co-founder, chairman, and CEO of Apple Inc. Through Apple, he is widely recognized as a charismatic pioneer of the personal computer revolution and for his influential career in the computer and consumer electronics fields, transforming "one industry after another, from computers and smart phones to music and movies". Jobs also co-founded and served as chief executive of Pixar Animation Studios; he became a member of the board of directors of The Walt Disney Company in 2006, when Disney acquired Pixar. Jobs was among the first to see the commercial potential of Xerox PARC's mouse-driven graphical user interface, which led to the creation of the Apple Lisa and, a year later, the Macintosh. He also played a role in introducing the LaserWriter, one of the first widely available laser printers, to the market.

James A. "Jim" Johnson (pg.202) - (September 10, 1912 – November 27, 2004) was an American football, basketball, and baseball player, coach, and college athletics administrator. He was tapped to reintroduce men's sports to East Carolina after World War II. He was the seventh head coach of the football, basketball and baseball teams at East Carolina Teachers College. He also was the athletic director for all sports teams. Before coaching, Johnson was a 16 letter winning athlete between 1933 to 1937. Johnson was inducted in 1978 into the ECU Hall of Fame.

-K-

Helen Adams Keller (pg.26, 96) - (June 27, 1880 – June 1, 1968) was an American author, political activist, and lecturer. She was the first deaf/blind person to earn a bachelor of arts degree. The story of how Keller's teacher, Anne Sullivan, broke through the isolation imposed by a near complete lack of language, allowing the girl to blossom as she learned to communicate, has become widely known through the dramatic depictions of the play and film The Miracle Worker. Her birthday on June 27 is commemorated as Helen Keller Day in the U.S. state of Pennsylvania and was authorized at the federal level by presidential proclamation by President Jimmy Carter in 1980, the 100th anniversary of her birth.

Robert Toru Kiyosaki (pg.100) - (born April 8, 1947) is an American investor, businessman, self-help author, motivational speaker, financial literacy activist, and financial commentator. Kiyosaki is well known for his Rich Dad Poor Dad series of motivational books and other material published under the Rich Dad brand. He has written over 15 books which have combined sales of over 26 million copies.

Raymond Albert "Ray" Kroc (pg.200) - (October 5, 1902 – January 14, 1984) was an American businessman of Czech origin. He joined McDonald's in 1954 and built it into the most successful fast food operation in the world. Kroc was included in Time 100: The Most Important People of the Century, and amassed a fortune during his lifetime. He owned the San Diego Padres baseball team from 1974 until his death in 1984. Similar to another fast-food giant, KFC founder Harland Sanders, Kroc's success came late in life when he was past his 50th birthday.

-L-

The Dalai Lama (pg.42, 212) - is a high lama in the Gelug or "yellow Hat" school of Tibetan Buddhism, founded by Tsongkhapa (1357–1419). The name is a combination of the Mongolic word dalai meaning "ocean" and the Tibetan word (bla-ma) meaning "guru, teacher, mentor".

Bruce Lee (pg.148) - (27 November 1940 – 20 July 1973) was a Hong Kong American martial artist, Hong Kong action film actor, martial arts instructor, filmmaker, and the founder of Jeet Kune Do. Lee was the son of Cantonese opera star Lee Hoi-Chuen. He is widely considered by commentators, critics, media and other martial artists to be one of the most influential martial artists of all time, and a pop culture icon of the 20th century. He is often credited with helping to change the way Asians were presented in American films.

Vincent Thomas "Vince" Lombardi (pg.80, 234) - (June 11, 1913 – September 3, 1970) was an American football player, coach, and executive. He is best known as the head coach of the Green Bay Packers during the 1960s, where he led the team to three straight and five total National Football League championships in seven years, including winning the first two Super Bowls following the 1966 and 1967 NFL seasons. Lombardi is considered by many to be one of the best and most successful coaches in NFL history. The National Football League's Super Bowl trophy is named in his honor. He was enshrined in the Pro Football Hall of Fame in 1971.

Tai Lopez (pg. 92) - is an investor, partner, or advisor to over 20 multi-million dollar businesses. Through his popular book club and podcasts Tai shares advice on how to achieve health, wealth, love, and happiness with 1.4 million people in 40 countries. In order to get feedback from an even larger audience, Tai started what is now one of the world's largest book clubs that reaches 1.4 million people in 40 countries with his "Book-Of-The-Day" free email newsletter. Tai recently summarized all he has learned from his mentors and compiled them into a series of 'mentor shortcuts' he calls, The 67 Steps. He also created an alternative to the traditional business school. This "Business Mentorship" program combines the best of self-learning with the best of a University degree without all the downsides of burdensome costs and inefficient methods. (www.TaiLopez.com)

-N-

Florence Nightingale (pg.44) - (12 May 1820 – 13 August 1910) was a celebrated English social reformer and statistician, and the founder of modern nursing. She came to prominence while serving as a nurse during the Crimean War, where she tended to wounded soldiers. She was known as "The Lady with the Lamp" after her habit of making rounds at night.

-P-

Dr. Norman Vincent Peale (pg.52) - (May 31, 1898 – December 24, 1993) was a minister and author (most notably of The Power of Positive Thinking) and a progenitor of "positive thinking".

Pablo Ruiz y Picasso (pg.98, 216) - also known as Pablo Picasso (25 October 1881 – 8 April 1973), was a Spanish painter, sculptor, print maker, ceramicist, stage designer, poet and playwright who spent most of his adult life in France. As one of the greatest and most influential artists of the 20th century, he is known for co-founding the Cubist movement, the invention of constructed sculpture, the co-invention of collage, and for the wide variety of styles that he helped develop and explore. Among his most famous works are the proto-Cubist Les Demoiselles d'Avignon (1907), and Guernica (1937), a portrayal of the German bombing of Guernica during the Spanish Civil War.

William Prescott (pg.118) - (February 20, 1726 – October 13, 1795) was an American colonel in the Revolutionary War who commanded the rebel forces in the Battle of Bunker Hill. Prescott is known for his order to his soldiers, "Do not fire until you see the whites of their eyes", such that the rebel troops may shoot at the enemy at shorter ranges, and therefore more accurately and lethally, and so conserve their limited stocks of ammunition. It is debated whether Prescott or someone earlier coined this memorable saying.

Chinese Proverb (pg.132, 168) - Chinese proverbs (yànyǔ) are famous sayings taken from literature, history, and famous people like philosophers. There are hundreds of Chinese proverbs addressing all aspects of life from education and work to personal goals and relationships. (From About. com)

Japanese Proverb (pg.164, 236) - The Japanese commonly use proverbs, often citing just the first part of common phrases for brevity. For example, one might say I no naka no kawazu (a frog in a well) to refer to the proverb I no naka no kawazu, taikai o shirazu (a frog in a well cannot conceive of the ocean?). Whereas proverbs in English are typically multi-worded phrases ("kill two birds with one stone"), Japanese yojijyukugo borrows from Chinese and compactly conveys the concept in one word Isseki nichou.

-R-

Ayn Rand (pg.206) - (February 2 or January 201905 – March 6, 1982) was an American novelist, philosopher, playwright, and screenwriter. She is known for her two best-selling novels, The Fountainhead and Atlas Shrugged, and for developing a philosophical system she called Objectivism. Born and educated in Russia, Rand moved to the United States in 1926. She had a play produced on Broadway in 1935–1936. After two early novels that were initially unsuccessful in America, she achieved fame with her 1943 novel, The Fountainhead.

Lucas J. Robak (pg.82, 180) – (born May 11, 1986) Lucas J. Robak graduated college in 2008 with a Bachelor of Science in Flight Operations and founded Melody of Life Foundation. After publishing a children's book, Lucas was diagnosed with multiple sclerosis (MS) influencing a change to the mission of his nonprofit in 2014. Within a year, Lucas co-authored another book; became a certified Master Practitioner of NLP, MER®, and Hypnotherapy; and published Master Your Life Using Transformational Quotes Workbook Series. As a selfless giver, Lucas wants people to reach their desired level of excellence. He's considered by many to be one of the most transformational and inspiring individuals today! (www.LucasRobak.com)

Anthony "Tony" Robbins (pg.188) - (born February 29, 1960) is an American life coach, self-help author and motivational speaker. He became well known through his infomercials and self-help books, Unlimited Power and Awaken the Giant Within. Robbins writes about subjects such as health and energy, overcoming fears, building wealth, persuasive communication, and enhancing relationships. Robbins began his career learning from many different motivational speakers, and promoted seminars for his personal mentor, Jim Rohn. He is deeply influenced by neuro-linguistic programming.

John Davison Rockefeller, Sr. (pg.176) - (July 8, 1839 – May 23, 1937) was an American business magnate and philanthropist. He was a co-founder of the Standard Oil Company, which dominated the oil industry and was the first great U.S. business trust. Rockefeller revolutionized the petroleum industry, and along with other key contemporary industrialists such as Andrew Carnegie, defined the structure of modern philanthropy. In 1870, he co-founded Standard Oil Company and actively ran it until he officially retired in 1897.

William Penn Adair "Will" Rogers (pg.178) - (November 4, 1879 – August 15, 1935) was an American cowboy, vaudeville performer, humorist, social commentator and motion picture actor. He was one of the world's best-known celebrities in the 1920s and 1930s.

Emanuel James (Jim) Rohn (pg.152, 186, 204) - (September 17, 1930 – December 5, 2009) was an American entrepreneur, author and motivational speaker. His rags to riches story played a large part in his work, which influenced others in the personal development industry.

Anna Eleanor Roosevelt (pg.84) - (October 11, 1884 – November 7, 1962) was an American politician. She was the longest-serving First Lady of the United States, holding the post from March 1933 to April 1945 during her husband President Franklin D. Roosevelt's four terms in office. President Harry S. Truman later called her the "First Lady of the World" in tribute to her human rights achievements.

Theodore "T.R." Roosevelt, Jr. (pg.66, 182) - (October 27, 1858 – January 6, 1919) was an American author, naturalist, explorer, historian, and politician who served as the 26th President of the United States. He was a leader of the Republican Party (the "GOP") and founder of the Progressive Party. He is noted for his exuberant personality, range of interests and achievements, and his leadership of the Progressive Movement, as well as his "cowboy" persona and robust masculinity. Born into a wealthy family in New York City, Roosevelt was a sickly child who suffered from asthma. To overcome his physical weakness, he embraced a strenuous life. He was home-schooled and became an eager student of nature. He attended Harvard University where he studied biology, boxed, and developed an interest in naval affairs. He entered politics in the New York state legislature, determined to become a member of the ruling class. In 1881, one year out of Harvard, he was elected to the New York State Assembly, where he became a leader of the reform faction of the GOP. His book The Naval War of 1812 (1882) established him as a learned historian and writer.

George Herman "Babe" Ruth, Jr. (pg.122) - (February 6, 1895 – August 16, 1948), nicknamed "the Bambino" and "the Sultan of Swat", was an American outfielder and pitcher who played 22 seasons in Major League Baseball (MLB), from 1914 to 1935. Beginning his career as a stellar left-handed pitcher for the Boston Red Sox, Ruth achieved his greatest fame as a slugging outfielder for the New York Yankees. He established many batting (and some pitching) records, including career home runs (714), slugging percentage (.690), runs batted in (RBIs) (2,213), bases on balls (2,062), and on-base plus slugging (OPS) (1.164), some of which have been broken. Ruth was one of the first five inductees into the National Baseball Hall of Fame in 1936.

-S-

Vaibhav Shah (pg.224) – Unable to locate a bio. If you find any information on Vaibhav Shah, please email the information to Lucas@LucasRobak.com

Jane Smiley (pg.22) - (born September 26, 1949) is an American novelist. Smiley published her first novel, Barn Blind, in 1980, and won a 1985 O. Henry Award for her short story "Lily", which was published in The Atlantic Monthly. Her best-selling A Thousand Acres, a story based on William Shakespeare's King Lear, received the Pulitzer Prize for Fiction in 1992. It was adapted into a film of the same title in 1997. In 1995 she wrote her sole television script, produced for an episode of Homicide: Life on the Street. Her novella The Age of Grief was made into the 2002 film The Secret Lives of Dentists. Her essay "Feminism Meets the Free Market" was included in the 2006 anthology Mommy Wars by Washington Post writer Leslie Morgan Steiner. Her essay "Why Bother?" appears in the anthology Knitting Yarns: Writers on Knitting, published by W. W. Norton & Company in 2013. Thirteen Ways of Looking at the Novel (2005), is a non-fiction meditation on the history and the nature of the novel, somewhat in the tradition of E. M. Forster's seminal Aspects of the Novel, that roams from eleventh century Japan's Murasaki Shikibu's The Tale of Genji to 21st-century American women's literature. In 2001, Smiley was elected a member of The American Academy of Arts and Letters. She participates in the annual Los Angeles Times Festival of Books in association with UCLA. Smiley chaired the judges' panel for the prestigious Man Booker International Prize in 2009.

William Clement Stone (pg.30) - (May 4, 1902 – September 3, 2002) was a businessman, philanthropist and New Thought self-help book author.

Charles Rozell "Chuck" Swindoll (pg.72) - (October 18, 1934-) is an evangelical Christian pastor, author, educator, and radio preacher. He founded Insight for Living, headquartered in Plano, Texas, which airs a radio program of the same name on more than 2,000 stations around the world in 15 languages.

-T-

Henry Major Tomlinson (pg.54) - (21 June 1873 – 5 February 1958) was a British writer and journalist. He was known for anti-war and travel writing, novels and short stories, especially of life at sea. He was born and died in London.

Mark Twain (pg.11, 56) - Samuel Langhorne Clemens - (November 30, 1835 – April 21, 1910), better known by his pen name Mark Twain, was an American author and humorist. He wrote The Adventures of Tom Sawyer (1876) and its sequel, Adventures of Huckleberry Finn (1885), the latter often called "the Great American Novel."

Lao Tzu (pg.166) - (Laozi) was a philosopher and poet of ancient China. He is best known as the reputed author of the Tao Te Ching and the founder of philosophical Taoism, but he is also revered as a deity in religious Taoism and traditional Chinese religions. Although a legendary figure, he is usually dated to around the 6th century BC and reckoned a contemporary of Confucius, but some historians contend that he actually lived during the Warring States period of the 5th or 4th century BC. A central figure in Chinese culture, Laozi is claimed by both the emperors of the Tang dynasty and modern common folk of the Li family as a founder of their lineage. Throughout history, Laozi's work has been embraced by various anti-authoritarian movements.

-V-

Colonel Norman Dane Vaughan (pg.102) - (December 19, 1905 – December 23, 2005) was an American dogsled driver and explorer whose first claim to fame was participating in Admiral Byrd's first expedition to the South Pole. He also mushed in a professional capacity as part of a search and rescue unit in World War II, in sporting events like the Olympics and the Iditarod Trail Sled Dog Race, and in three Presidential Inauguration ceremonies.

-W-

Denis E. Waitley (pg.76, 154) - (born 1933), is an American motivational speaker and writer, consultant and best-selling author. Waitley is a graduate of the U.S. Naval Academy at Annapolis. He was a founding member of the National Council for Self-Esteem. He has authored 16 books and has released hundreds of audio lectures.

Booker Taliaferro Washington (pg.146) - (April 5, 1856 – November 14, 1915) was an African-American educator, author, orator, and adviser to presidents of the United States. Between 1890 and 1915, Washington was the dominant leader in the African-American community.

Oprah Gail Winfrey (pg.36) - (born January 29, 1954) is an American media proprietor, talk show host, actress, producer, and philanthropist. Winfrey is best known for her multi-award-winning talk show The Oprah Winfrey Show which was the highest-rated program of its kind in history and was nationally syndicated from 1986 to 2011. Dubbed the "Queen of All Media", she has been ranked the richest African-American of the 20th century, the greatest black philanthropist in American history, and is currently North America's only black billionaire. She is also, according to some assessments, the most influential woman in the world. In 2013, she was awarded the Presidential Medal of Freedom by President Barack Obama and an honorary doctorate degree from Harvard.

John Robert Wooden (pg.46, 70) - (October 14, 1910 – June 4, 2010) was an American basketball player and coach. Nicknamed the "Wizard of Westwood," as head coach at UCLA he won ten NCAA national championships in a 12-year period—seven in a row — an unprecedented feat. Within this period, his teams won a record 88 consecutive games. He was named national coach of the year six times.

-Z-

Zig Ziglar (pg.68) – Hilary Hinton "Zig" Ziglar (November 6, 1926 – November 28, 2012) was an American author, salesman, and motivational speaker.

Will you become someone worth citing?

ABOUT
LUCAS J. ROBAK

After making wine and flying airplanes, Lucas discovered what he was born for. While laying on a hospital bed a team on neurologists handed him his life's purpose on a silver platter.

Being diagnosed with multiple sclerosis (MS) helped him finally realize that he's here to help people become aware of health and wellness.

Soon enough, Lucas was an organizer for *The Wellness Fair* to connect accredited wellness professionals with those who desire complete well-being.

Before all this happened, while reading a book to a friend's son, Lucas decided anyone can write a book. To prove this, a year later parents began reading his first book to their kids, *I AM – Children's Book for Positive Thinkers*.

This fun experiment found its way into Bob Proctor's legendary personal library and is being read to Jack Canfield's grandson.

Because people were asking, in one calendar year, Lucas published 75 people around the world for fun. Seeing what a book can do for someone, he now works with wellness professionals to get their book published so they can reach more people.

As a multi #1 international bestselling author and a contributor to numerous publications like *Addicted 2 Success*, *Good Men Project*, and *Thrive Global*, Lucas also has been interviewed on many podcasts and TV shows about his story and expertise.

Anything and everything is possible as long as you truly desire it. Remember this!

Be Different! Be You!

Lucas J. Robak

www.LucasRobak.com
Lucas@LucasRobak.com

OTHER BOOKS
BY LUCAS J. ROBAK

Master Your Life: Transformational Quotes Workbook Series

Take a journey to find your lost passions and use them to fulfill your ultimate life purpose. Empower and enrich your life through extraordinary words of achievement and success. Use this workbook series as a guide to live your passions, define your optimal outcomes.

I AM: Children's Book for Positive Thinkers

By the time our children reach seven years old, their perception about themselves is already set. Before we reach the age of eighteen, we'll have been told negative limiting beliefs over 17,000 times. Use this book to instill positive thinking in the minds of your whole family.

The One Minute Authorpreneur: Entrepreneur Publishing Series

By using a book as a marketing tool, you can leverage it in many different ways to achieve your desires. Instantly separate yourself from the competition by positioning yourself as the subject matter expert. As an authorpreneur, selling books isn't important when compared to how the book sells you. #1minAuthor

www.LucasRobak.com/Products

www.ingramcontent.com/pod-product-compliance
Lightning Source LLC
Chambersburg PA
CBHW030916090426
42737CB00007B/211